*Moments of Peace*
*in the Presence of God*

PRESENTED TO:

PRESENTED BY:

DATE:

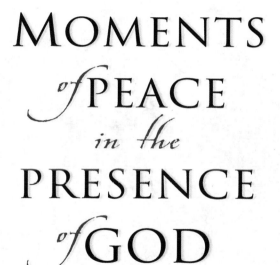

# MOMENTS *of* PEACE *in the* PRESENCE *of* GOD

*Reflections on
God's Gift
of Love, Hope,
and Happiness*

# MOMENTS
*of* PEACE

*in the*

# PRESENCE
*of* GOD

BETHANYHOUSE
MINNEAPOLIS, MINNESOTA

*Moments of Peace in the Presence of God*
Copyright © 2004 by GRQ Ink, Inc.
Brentwood, Tennessee 37027

Published by Bethany House Publishers
11400 Hampshire Avenue South
Bloomington, Minnesota 55438
www.bethanyhouse.com

Bethany House Publishers is a Division of Baker Book House Company, Grand Rapids, Michigan.

Library of Congress Control Number 2003024009
ISBN 0-7642-2922-2

Compiler and Editor: Lila Empson
Writers: Phillip H. Barnhart, Jan Coleman, Angela J. Kiesling, Margaret Langstaff, Karen O'Connor, and representatives of Snapdragon Editorial Group, Inc.
Design: Diane Whisner

04 05 06    4 3 2 1

Seek the LORD and his strength;
seek his presence continually

PSALM 105:4 NRSV

# CONTENTS

Introduction .................... 12

The Light of God's Love .................... 16

Mended Heart .................... 18

A Flame Rekindled .................... 20

Never Alone .................... 22

A Personal Passage .................... 24

Plenty of Time .................... 26

Hope and Humility .................... 28

Promises to Keep .................... 30

Someone to Count On .................... 32

True Happiness .................... 34

A New Song .................... 36

Woven in Secret .................... 38

Searching for Answers .................... 40

Safe and Sound .................... 42

An Enduring Peace .................... 46

A Steady Guide .................... 48

Second Chances .................... 50

Seeking Success .................... 52

Sharing God's Compassion .................... 54

Settled in Heaven .................... 56

Beginning Again .................... 58

God's Fix for Fear .................... 60

Facing the Sunlight .................... 62

God's Majesty .................... 64

Someone to Live For .................... 66

Answered Prayers .................... 68

The Kite String .................... 70

God Shares Your Cares .................... 72

True North .................... 76

The Master Plan .................... 78

A New Way of Thinking .................... 80

Questions and Doubts .................... 82

What Really Matters .................... 84

Wonder and Awe .................... 86

A Bright New Day .................... 88

Simply Believe .................... 90

Winning Over Worry .................... 92

The Work of Waiting .................... 94

Pausing for Power .................... 96

Taking Hold of Grace .................... 98

Returning to Life .................... 100

More Than Enough .................... 102

Desert Streams
.................... 106

The Cost of Commitment
.................... 108

The Eyes of Understanding
.................... 110

Divine Destiny
.................... 112

A Wealth of Wisdom
.................... 114

Mysterious Ways
.................... 116

Facing the Future
.................... 118

Rising to the Challenge
.................... 120

Songs for the Soul
.................... 122

Ice Storms
.................... 124

Leaping for Joy
.................... 126

Autumn Leaves
.................... 128

Staying Steady Through
Tough Times
.................... 130

God Is on the Throne
.................... 132

A Pattern of Patience
.................... 136

Wings of Mercy
.................... 138

Sure Footing
.................... 140

The Source of Hope
.................... 142

God's Faithfulness
.................... 144

Seeking and Yearning for God
.................... 146

God's Joy and Delight in
Your Life
.................... 148

Comfort in God
.................... 150

Loving God
.................... 152

God's Mercy and Compassion
.................... 154

God's Power, Presence, and Peace
.................... 156

God's Greatness and Majesty
.................... 158

God Listens to Your Prayers
.................... 160

Prayer Banishes Worry and Fear
.................... 162

Prayer Helps You Make Decisions
.................... 166

The Lord Wants to Use Your
Talents
.................... 168

Faith, Hope, and Love
.................... 170

God Is in the Details
.................... 172

The Kingdom of God Is Now
.................... 174

God Is Love
.................... 176

God Reveals Himself in
Your Daily Life
.................... 178

Your Hope Is in God
.................... 180

Patience as You Wait on the Lord
.................... 182

The Gift of Giving
.................... 184

Making a Sanctuary for the Spirit
.................... 186

The Lord Renews and Refreshes
Your Life
.................... 188

All Creation Praises God
.................... 190

Prayer in a Dry Season
.................... 192

The Divine Mystery at the Heart of Life .......................... 196

God's Love Makes You Wealthy .......................... 198

Accepting the Lord's Guidance .......................... 200

Finding Your Life in God .......................... 202

Believe in Miracles .......................... 204

Shh, Listen .......................... 206

At Peace With the World in God .......................... 208

The Forgiving Heart .......................... 210

God's Tender Mercies .......................... 212

A Time for Rest .......................... 214

Joy .......................... 216

Heaven .......................... 220

Your Thankfulness and Praise to God .......................... 222

God's Direction and Correction .......................... 224

God Lightens Your Cares and Burdens .......................... 226

The Discipline of Daily Prayer .......................... 228

Inviting God Into Your Home .......................... 230

God Dispels Confusion and Doubt .......................... 232

Grace Sufficient for the Hour .......................... 234

Claiming God's Blessings .......................... 236

People Are to Be Helped, Not Shunned .......................... 238

The Healing Power of God .......................... 240

When Clouds Come .......................... 242

Taking the Roll .......................... 244

A New Name .......................... 246

Out of Harm's Way .......................... 248

God's Eraser .......................... 250

Everywhere You Are .......................... 252

A Steadfast Heart .......................... 256

The Beauty of Change .......................... 258

Stoking the Fire .......................... 260

A Childlike Contentment .......................... 262

The Gift of Forgiveness .......................... 264

A Decision to Trust .......................... 266

No Fear! .......................... 268

The Confidence of Answered Prayer .......................... 270

An Eternal Perspective .......................... 272

God Satisfies the Soul .......................... 274

Finding Favor With God .......................... 276

Strength and Courage .......................... 278

The Shepherd's Leading .......................... 280

Rest for the Weary .......................... 282

Inspiration on High ............ 286

Thirsting for God ............ 288

The Blessedness of Helping ............ 290

The Refiner's Fire ............ 292

Hope's Reward ............ 294

Delight in His Will ............ 296

Reaping the Joy ............ 298

Fortified in Spirit ............ 300

The Divine Gatekeeper ............ 302

Healing the Broken Heart ............ 304

Waiting for God's Timing ............ 306

Praise in the Evening ............ 308

The Amazing Grace of God ............ 310

Traveling Mercies ............ 312

Growing Wiser ............ 316

Divine Nourishment ............ 318

Taking Refuge in Strength ............ 320

Distinct and Beautiful ............ 322

Hidden in the Secret Place ............ 324

Nature: God's Herald ............ 326

Joy of the Bridegroom ............ 328

The Blessings of Long Life ............ 330

Reason for Rejoicing ............ 332

Sweeter Than Honey ............ 334

God's Perfect Plan ............ 336

The Message in the Gates ............ 338

Lord of the Night ............ 340

Lord of the Light ............ 342

Renewed Vigor ............ 346

Tears in a Bottle ............ 348

Personal Memorials ............ 350

God's Awesome Deeds ............ 352

Words That Restore ............ 354

Joy in Lowly Tasks ............ 356

The Teachable Heart ............ 358

God's Strength Is Enough ............ 360

God's Answer Is on the Way ............ 362

God's Mercy ............ 364

A Bountiful Crop ............ 366

A Time to Be Loud ............ 368

Along the Footpath ............ 370

A Lasting Heritage ............ 372

Wholesome Preservatives ............ 374

Someone Better Than Before ............ 376

God's Night Watch ............ 378

Skillfully Wrought ............ 380

# INTRODUCTION

When Jesus went to his disciples on the evening of his resurrection, the first thing he said to them was, "Peace be with you."

That has not changed. When you are in the presence of God, you are in a place of peace. Peace

comes from the presence of someone who made you in love and keeps you in grace, someone you can count on to be with you in all things. When you are in God's presence, you are with one who knows you better than anyone does and who wants you to have the best life has to offer. In such a

presence you have an inner calm that exceeds human understanding and measurement.

This book invites you into the presence of God, where the gift of peace awaits. In its pages you can discover that God is nearer to you than you are to yourself. To know God's presence in this way is to be at peace.

The LORD will give strength
to His people;
The LORD will bless His
people with peace.

Psalm 29:11  NASB

# faith hope

moments of peace in the presence of God

*love*

*Truly the eye of the
LORD is on those
who fear him, on
those who hope
in his steadfast love.*

PSALM 33:18 NRSV

*hope*

# THE LIGHT OF GOD'S LOVE

*The LORD is God, and he has made his light shine upon us.*

PSALM 118:27 NIV

Problems always seem most daunting just before the dawn—right before the morning  light climbs above the horizon and slips quietly into the room. In that darkest hour, shadows of fear and discouragement may threaten to overwhelm you. But the morning light chases away the nighttime, restoring your perspective, filling you with hope, and offering you the promise of a bright new day!

The light of God's love is much like the morning sunlight. It dispels darkness from your heart and sweeps away shadows of fear and discouragement. It renders harmless specters of condemnation that would harshly remind you of past failures. God's wondrous light allows you to see yourself as he sees you—a new creature, forgiven, ready to begin again.

The LORD is my light and my salvation; whom shall I fear? The LORD is the strength of my life; of whom shall I be afraid?

PSALM 27:1 KJV

God, I thank you for flooding my heart with the light of your love and for illuminating the shadows and bringing a bright, shining morning of hope to my life. Amen.

# MENDED HEART

*The LORD is close to the brokenhearted
and saves those who are crushed in spirit.*

PSALM 34:18 NIV

Few people pass through life without feeling the sting of betrayal, the loss of friendship, or the failure of important relationships. At those times, you may feel that the pain of a broken heart will cling to you for the rest of your days and that you will never be whole again. Sometimes you may even wonder if God still loves you.

God does love you, purely, simply, and unconditionally. Even if your pain is the result of your own actions, God's love does not condemn you. It urges you forward, calling you to forgive yourself, make amends, and become a better person. His love is constant and predictable. And with the assurance of his love comes hope—hope that you will love again, trust again, offer your heart again.

My flesh and my heart
faileth: but God is the
strength of my heart,
and my portion for ever.

PSALM 73:26 KJV

Thank you, God, for the promise of your constant love and
the hope it brings to my life.
Amen.

# A FLAME REKINDLED

*I wait for the LORD, my soul waits, and in his word I hope.*

PSALM 130:5 NRSV

A blazing wood fire is glorious, but when it's spent, nothing remains but white-gray ash—

 a somber contrast to the rough-cut log that once lay on the hearth and the colorful flames that danced high in the air, filling the room with warmth.

At times you may feel that your life is reduced to ashes, that your strength is gone, and that the flame you once carried inside is cold and colorless. But God promises that even at your lowest point, even when you feel there is nothing left with which to rebuild your life, he is there to rekindle the flame within you. His indwelling Spirit offers hope and strength for you to begin again, and his never-failing love shines brightly on your path, illuminating each step you take.

Why am I discouraged? Why so sad? I will put my hope in God!

PSALM 43:5 NLT

God, I thank you that the fire of your Spirit brings new life to my body and soul. I will place my life in your hands and my hope in your faithfulness and love. Amen.

# NEVER ALONE

*I am continually with thee: thou hast holden me by my right hand. Thou shalt guide me with thy counsel, and afterward receive me to glory.*

PSALM 73:23–24 KJV

A solitary tree standing in the middle of a field may appear to be deserted by all else. In fact, however, it is not. The warmth of the sun kisses that tree; the gentle breezes caress it; the fellowship of birds on the wing gladden it; and a small underground universe of lively creatures stimulate it.

At some time in your life you experience loneliness. Loneliness is natural and should be appreciated rather than feared. In seasons of loneliness, you discover that you are never truly alone—no more than that solitary tree. People you barely notice during times of social prosperity surround you and can become valuable friends. But the greatest discovery is that God is constantly with you, warming you with his love, and you can learn to hope in him.

I love the LORD because he hears and answers my prayers. Because he bends down and listens, I will pray as long as I have breath!

PSALM 116:1–2 NLT

God, during those times when I feel the ache of loneliness, help me to remember that you are never more than a whispered prayer away. Amen.

# A PERSONAL PASSAGE

*He reached down from on high and took hold of
me; he drew me out of deep waters.*

PSALM 18:16 NIV

Each life is a journey—a uniquely personal
passage through time. As you
travel through difficult places,
you need not give in to hopelessness. God is able to bring you
safely to your destination when
you place your trust in him.

God is the Author of each
journey. He knows the way through every dark
and frightening valley. He knows the safest path
along each high and treacherous mountain trail.
God knows where the cool, refreshing waters
flow and where you can find the provisions to
meet each of your needs. He shares the weight
of the burden you carry and causes you to lie
down and rest in lush green meadows. He gives
you hope and courage as you walk with him,
step by step, one day at a time.

You will show me the way of life, granting me the joy of your presence and the pleasures of living with you forever.

PSALM 16:11 NLT

God, as I face the challenges of my personal journey through life, I am thankful for your presence that guides and protects me.
Amen.

# PLENTY OF TIME

*A thousand years mean nothing to you! They are merely a day gone by or a few hours in the night.*

PSALM 90:4 CEV

Time is both an enemy and a friend. You do your best to conquer it, and yet it continually slips through your fingers. You measure your life, your successes, and your productivity in terms of minutes, hours, days, and weeks. You often lose your hope in the future and in the fulfillment of your dreams as time passes.

God isn't subject to your concept of time, for he is the Master of the universe. When you place your trust in him, you can know with certainty that you have all the time you need to do what he has created you to do and that you have plenty of time to become all that he created you to be. Your brightest hour is always ahead, never behind!

LORD, I trust you. I have
said, "You are my God."
My life is in your hands.

PSALM 31:14–15 NCV

I place my seconds, minutes,
hours, and days in your hands,
God. I thank you for restoring
my hope in the future.
Amen.

# HOPE AND HUMILITY

*Though the LORD is supreme,*
*he takes care of those who are humble,*
*but he stays away from the proud.*

PSALM 138:6 NCV

Many people believe that such things as money, possessions, good looks, intelligence, and even power are the measure of their lives. None of these is inherently bad, yet none can predict happiness or instill a lasting sense of worth. What if you were to awaken one morning to find that your personal wealth and power had vanished? What if your attractiveness failed and your intelligence faltered? Would hopelessness and despair overcome you?

God places little importance on outward appearances or the size of bank accounts. He measures your life and hearts by a different standard. He teaches you that humility leads to greatness and that you achieve true success when you give yourselves to others. No measure other than the eternal love of God is a true measure.

God, examine me and know my heart; test me and know my nervous thoughts. See if there is any bad thing in me. Lead me on the road to everlasting life.

PSALM 139:23–24 NCV

God, help me measure my life by your standard so that my hope may shine brightly and never be disappointed. Amen.

# PROMISES TO KEEP

*My eyes stay open through the watches of the night, that I may meditate on your promises.*
PSALM 119:148 NIV

What would life be like without spring's warmth after a long and cold winter, rest after an exhausting and difficult day, achievement after an intense and tiring struggle? Promises of the reward to come mark your life. In fact, life is a promise in the process of being kept.

You may wonder at times if your life is no longer a bright promise. You may lie awake in the night hours rehearsing your regrets that this may be so. But God is the great promise keeper. You can count on what he has promised. He is already aware of every poor choice, every lost opportunity, and every wasted second. He knows, and your mistakes grieve him. He takes you as you are and restores hope to your life.

Your promise revives me; it comforts me in all my troubles.

PSALM 119:50 NLT

God, I will focus my eyes on your faithfulness rather than on my own failures. I will look to you to help me fulfill the promise of all that my life can be. Amen.

# SOMEONE TO COUNT ON

*I have been young, and now am old; yet have I not seen the righteous forsaken, nor his seed begging bread.*

PSALM 37:25 KJV

Life is a long and complex journey that includes the tragic and the sublime, the good times and the bad times. Where can you turn when the bad times come? Who will keep your feet from stumbling when your eyes are filled with tears?

Even your closest friends and family can disappoint you—just as you can disappoint them. You can be confident that there is someone who will never let you down, someone who will be there for you in every season of your life, someone who will lift your burdens and provide light for your feet as you walk along dark and lonely stretches of life's road. That someone is God. He has promised never to leave you nor forsake you. He will walk with you every step of the way.

Keep me safe, O God, for in you I take refuge.

PSALM 16:1 NIV

God, thank you for the comforting light of your presence and the comforting strength of your arm that lead me carefully through the dark places in my life. Amen.

# TRUE HAPPINESS

*Happy is he that hath the God of Jacob for his help, whose hope is in the LORD his God.*

PSALM 146:5 KJV

Everyone pursues happiness, but few can define it. Is happiness the bright red apple dan-

gling from the highest branch of the tree or the immense treasure buried somewhere underground? Is happiness the perfect person with whom to spend your life? Many times you lose hope of finding happiness simply because you may be looking for it in the wrong places.

True happiness has less to do with outward circumstances than with inward, and more to do with inward harmony than with outward. True happiness is being anchored to your Creator, who knows you better than you know yourself. True happiness isn't dependent on another person. It isn't dangling out of your reach or hiding deep underground. True happiness can be found in the ordinary activities of your life. You need only look inward and upward.

Happy are those who respect the LORD and obey him. You will enjoy what you work for, and you will be blessed with good things.

PSALM 128:1–2 NCV

God, as I lay my search at your feet, restore my hope of finding true and lasting happiness. Amen.

# A NEW SONG

*He hath put a new song in my mouth, even*
*praise unto our God: many shall see it, and fear,*
*and shall trust in the Lord.*

PSALM 40:3 KJV

Your journey through life is not often easy, and you may experience times when you awaken to find yourself battered and bruised, lost and forsaken, lying helpless along the side of life's road. Your resources gone and your strength spent, you may wonder if there is hope for you. Will anyone come along to help?

God has promised that there is no circumstance from which he cannot rescue you. If you call out to him, he will help you to your feet and provide comfort and support until your wounds heal and you are able to continue on your way. Though the circumstances that caused your fall may still be present, he has promised to walk with you, steadying your feet and filling your heart with hope until you reach your final destination.

You will help me, LORD God,
and keep me from falling.

PSALM 54:4 CEV

I have no strength left, God.
Lift me up and give me new
hope as I place my trust in you.
Amen.

# WOVEN IN SECRET

*My frame was not hidden from you when I was made in the secret place. When I was woven together in the depths of the earth, your eyes saw my unformed body.*

PSALM 139:15–16 NIV

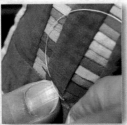

A butterfly slips slowly from its cocoon and flutters away on a gentle breeze. Hidden from sight, it passes through a transforming process known only to God, its Creator. In the same way that God made the butterfly, God fashioned you in secret—adding, subtracting, and shaping as only the great Creator can.

When you are tempted to question your inherent worth or to see yourself as ugly and ungainly, you must remember that you are a treasured piece of God's own handiwork. You are an expression of the same creative force that placed the stars in the sky, strewed the flowers along the path, and raised up dry land in the midst of the sea. It is in the hand of the Artist that you have reason to hope.

He brought me out into a
broad place; he delivered me,
because he delighted in me.

PSALM 18.19 NRSV

Great Creator, when my failings
cause me to lose a sense of my
own value, I will hope in you,
for you made me.
Amen.

# SEARCHING FOR ANSWERS

*I look up to the mountains; does my strength come from mountains? No, my strength comes from GOD, who made heaven, and earth, and mountains.*

PSALM 121:1 THE MESSAGE

Answers to some questions are difficult to find. Why are you here? What purpose does your life serve? Why is the life of a child cut short? Why is a strong and decent man cut down in his prime? Why must a young mother care for her children alone? Why do evil people prosper? Why do the ravages of war seem never to end?

You may never know the answers to these questions or the thousands of others drawn from the circumstances of your life and from those around you. You can but place your hand in the hand of God and place your hope in his great wisdom and eternal love. You can rest in the knowledge that his intention for you is always good.

I truly believe I will live to
see the LORD's goodness.

PSALM 27:13 NCV

God, settle my heart and help
me to rest in the hope that
one day all my questions will
be answered as I stand in
your presence.
Amen.

# SAFE AND SOUND

*You will not fear the terror of the night, or the arrow that flies by day.*

PSALM 91:5 NRSV

The eyes of the mother lion never leave her cubs as they scuffle playfully in the under-

brush. Her instinct to guard and protect her little ones is intense and constant. She leaves them only long enough to secure food in the darkest hours of the night.

God watches over you more carefully than the most attentive lioness watches over her cubs. His eyes are on you as you move through your days. Under his constant watchfulness, you can find safety and wholeness. In the midst of danger and chaos, you will find that his presence is a source of hope and peace. When you call on him for help, be assured that he will come quickly to rescue you and show you the way to safety.

The LORD will keep you
from all evil; he will
keep your life.

PSALM 121:7 NRSV

I often feel fearful and inse-
cure as I search for safety and
protection for those I love
and for me. From this day
forward, I will place my trust
in you, God, and hope in
your faithfulness and love.
Amen.

# faith hope

moments of peace in the presence of God

*love*

In peace I will both
lie down and sleep,
For You alone, O
LORD, make me to
dwell in safety.

PSALM 4:8 NASB

*peace*

# AN ENDURING PEACE

*Great peace have they which love thy law: and nothing shall offend them.*

PSALM 119:165 KJV

The starry grandeur of a midsummer night. The gentle gurgle of a languid river. The majestic stillness of a desert vista. The rolling wave of unharvested grain. The cleansing rain on a warm day. These are but a few of the natural expressions of peace and constancy that God has placed in the world.

In times of turmoil and distress, you can find moments of comfort and solace by gazing at the ageless beauty of a snowcapped mountain or by walking along a shell-strewn beach. For a while you enjoy the sense of peace. You hope that when you return to your everyday life the peace you found will remain with you. God alone can offer you lasting peace; only he can establish that lasting peace in your heart.

You make the springs pour water into ravines, so streams gush down from the mountains. They provide water for all the animals, and the wild donkeys quench their thirst. The birds nest beside the streams and sing among the branches of the trees.

PSALM 104:10–12 NLT

God, bring peace and constancy to my heart, where pain and hopelessness now reside. I will hope in your goodness.
Amen.

# A STEADY GUIDE

*Show me your ways, O LORD, teach me your paths; guide me in your truth and teach me, for you are God my Savior, and my hope is in you all day long.*

PSALM 25:4–5 NIV

As you travel through unmarked trails and uncharted valleys of life, you may sometimes become disoriented and lose your way. Feeling lost and alone, you may be tempted to give up and abandon your dreams and ambitions.

When you lose your hope in the future, you grieve the heart of God. It is his desire to be your steady guide, to take each of you by the hand and lead you through the tangled underbrush. He longs to walk with you each step of the way, pointing out the dangers and keeping your feet securely on the path. I'll never leave you, he tells you. I'll illuminate your path with the light of my love. No matter how lost and disoriented you become, God is always available to help you find your way again.

God is our protection and
our strength. He always
helps in times of trouble.

PSALM 46:1 NCV

God, as I travel through this
life, I will take your hand and
trust you to lead me safely
through each day.
Amen.

# SECOND CHANCES

*The LORD has mercy on those who respect him,*
*as a father has mercy on his children.*

PSALM 103:13 NCV

Mistakes are inevitable; everyone makes them at some time or another. Sometimes the

consequences of these mistakes are far-reaching, even irreversible. You may feel you are doomed to a life of frustration and despair, enslaved by the misdeeds of the past and the shadows of yesterday. In those difficult

times, you can turn for help to the God of the rainbow, the God of second chances.

Even when your mistakes are so devastating that you cannot return to the life you once knew, God's light can break through the threatening clouds and splash spectacular color across your life. The consequences of your actions cannot be reversed, but God can add his miraculous touch and help you to build something new and uniquely beautiful. You only need to ask.

He brought me up also out of
an horrible pit, out of the
miry clay, and set my feet
upon a rock, and established
my goings.

PSALM 40:2 KJV

You are the God of second
chances. Grace my life with
the miracle of your touch,
and help me to begin again
beneath the rainbow of
your faithful love.
Amen.

# SEEKING SUCCESS

*Deal bountifully with your servant, so that I may live and observe your word.*

PSALM 119:17 NRSV

*Success* means different things to different people. To one the word means wealth

and fame; to another it means comfort and contentment; to yet another it means accomplishment and fulfillment. You measure success by the degree to which you obtain the things that are most important to you.

But even when you achieve the goals you've set, you sometimes arrive at the finish line only to feel that your victory is empty and meaningless. Too late you realize that your furious run was in the wrong direction, and you experience feelings of sorrow and regret. God measures success in terms of faith, hope, and love. It is never too late to begin following his lead. Your consequent victory will bring lasting satisfaction and a sense of true success.

Lead me in the path of your commands, because that makes me happy. Make me want to keep your rules instead of wishing for riches. Keep me from looking at worthless things. Let me live by your word.

PSALM 119:35–37 NCV

Help me, God, to measure success by your standard, trusting you to keep me headed in the right direction. Amen.

# SHARING GOD'S COMPASSION

*He, being full of compassion, forgave their iniquity, and destroyed them not: yea, many a time turned he his anger away, and did not stir up all his wrath.*

PSALM 78:38 KJV

Compassion does not exist in the natural world. A sudden wind uproots a tree with no regard for its usefulness. A boulder slips from its perch and crushes the flowers that flourish peacefully at its base. A stormy sea swallows a ship with no regard for the souls on board. Compassion is a characteristic that flows only from the heart of God.

The words and actions of others may hurt you. When you respond with a heart of compassion, however, you demonstrate that you are God's child. God has compassion on you even if you turn your back to him, and he extends his hand to help you when you are lost and without hope. In the same way, you show your godlikeness by letting his compassion flow through you to others.

You, O LORD, are a compassionate and gracious God,
slow to anger, abounding in
love and faithfulness.

PSALM 86:15 NIV

Thank you, God, for pouring
out your compassion on me.
And thank you for allowing
me to share that compassion
with others.
Amen.

# SETTLED IN HEAVEN

*I will never stop loving him, nor let my promise
to him fail. No, I will not break my covenant; I
will not take back a single word I said.*

PSALM 89:33–34 NLT

Each life has its share of disappointments—those dark moments
when something you were
counting on fails to materialize
or when someone you believe in
lets you down. When you are
struggling with the uncertainty
that people and plans bring to
your life, it is a great comfort to know that
God will never fail you and that every plan he
sets in place will prosper.

As you travel through the dark places on
your journey through life, that old bandit disappointment may jump from the shadows and
challenge you, threatening to rob you of your
dreams. But disappointment cannot take what
is yours as long as you remember that you are
a child of God. With God on your side, your
future is secure and settled in heaven.

The LORD looks at the world
from his throne in heaven,
and he watches us all.

PSALM 33:13–14 CEV

God, thank you for the one
true thing in my life—your
faithful love. Help me to
place my hope in you.
Amen.

# BEGINNING AGAIN

*The steps of a good man are ordered by the
LORD: and he delighteth in his way. Though he
fall, he shall not be utterly cast down: for the
LORD upholdeth him with his hand.*

PSALM 37:23–24 KJV

A tiny shoot thrusts itself through the crusty soil and pushes up into the sunlight. Fragile but determined, it presses on until one day it is covered with beautiful flowers. It stands glorious in triumph—until the cold winter winds extinguish its beauty and strip it of all it has worked so hard to accomplish. But the story does not end. In season, spring breezes blow across the forsaken ground and the sun once again warms the earth. Its hope restored, the little shoot, waiting beneath the soil, begins its journey again.

In many ways, your life is as fragile as that tiny plant. Cold winds may blow over you, leaving you feeling withered and ruined. But then God shines his light on your life and you can blossom once more.

Faithfulness will spring up
from the ground, and righteousness will look down
from the sky.

PSALM 85:11 NRSV

God, help me push through
the crusty soil of heartache
and bloom again in the
springtime of your love.
Amen.

# GOD'S FIX FOR FEAR

*The LORD is my light and my salvation; Whom shall I fear? The LORD is the strength of my life; Of whom shall I be afraid?*

PSALM 27:1 NKJV

Fear is a predator. It crouches in the shadows and stalks its prey, you, waiting for any sign of weakness or vulnerability on your part. When fear strikes, it can ravage your life. It is a fierce and deadly enemy. Fear can rob you of family and relationships, destroy your talent, and wipe out your resources.

God has given you a mighty sword with which to fight the predator fear—your faith. Faith protects you from fear's torment and allows you to face each new day with hope and confidence. Faith frees you to tackle the real obstacles in your life rather than to waste your energies dealing with difficulties that might never materialize. Your faith in God gives you the courage to face fear and drive it away.

O God, I praise your word.
I trust in God, so why should
I be afraid? What can mere
mortals do to me?

PSALM 56:4 NLT

Thank you, God, for the gift
of faith that brings me hope
and drives fear away.
Amen.

# FACING THE SUNLIGHT

*The LORD God is a sun and shield: the LORD*
*will give grace and glory: no good thing will he*
*withhold from them that walk uprightly.*

PSALM 84:11 KJV

 At times your life is filled with the dark-
ness of a polar night, with icy
winds blowing across the frozen
reaches of your heart. In these
times, you must place your hope in
God, for he will not allow the icy
darkness to reign forever in your
life. Eventually the sun will shine
again, melting your ice-locked
emotions.

The promise of renewed life comes with
the sunlight of his love. You feel an unre-
strained urge to turn your face upward into its
brilliance. The sunlight illuminates your heart
and chases away the long, cold night. You find
that once again you are able to love and laugh
and live; once again you are able to appreciate
the good things God has placed in your life.
His mercy has wrought a bright, new morning.

Light is sown for the righteous, and gladness for the
upright in heart.

PSALM 97:11 KJV

God, thank you for bringing
sunlight to my soul and
warming my frozen heart.
Amen.

# GOD'S MAJESTY

*Honor and majesty are before Him;*
*Strength and beauty are in His sanctuary.*

PSALM 96:6 NKJV

God's majesty crowns the earth and the heavens. It is reflected in the splendor of the nighttime sky and the expanse of the ocean. It is echoed in the strength of the mountains and the might of a river. It is evident in every loving gesture and simple act of forgiveness.

In times of loneliness and heartache, the visible signs of God's majesty bring us comfort, for they do more than decorate his greatness. They express his power, his constancy, and his resourcefulness—all available to us in our time of need. They remind us that our God is great and loving and kind, that our God is faithful and powerful enough to heal our broken hearts and to give us the will to go on.

It was you who opened up
springs and streams; you
dried up the ever flowing
rivers. The day is yours,
and yours also the night;
you established the sun
and moon.

PSALM 74:15–16 NIV

Great God of the Universe,
when I look around me and
see your majesty, I will
rejoice in the fact that your
mighty hand is extended
toward me. I will place
my hope in you.
Amen.

# SOMEONE TO LIVE FOR

*Just tell me what to do and I will do it, Lord. As long as I live I'll wholeheartedly obey. Make me walk along the right paths for I know how delightful they really are.*

PSALM 119:33–35 TLB

Tragedy, disaster, adversity, calamity, trauma, loss. You can be left struggling with questions. Can any good come from your suffering? How could that happen? Can anyone take your confusion and make sense of it all? Is that possible? Can anyone turn your life around and make it worth living? Oh, that it were so.

When you ask if there is something to live for, God wants you to know that there is someone to live for—God. You can live for God, because he can take your confusion and anger and create something beautiful. He can wash away your loneliness and redeem your losses. He can bring meaning to your life simply by reminding you that you are created in his image.

O taste and see that the LORD is good; happy are those who take refuge in him.

PSALM 34:8 NRSV

God, thank you for the meaning and purpose you bring to my life. Thank you for allowing me to surrender my sorrow to you so that you can replace it with hope and happiness. I can truly live for you. Amen.

# ANSWERED PRAYERS

*Praise God, who did not ignore my prayer or hold back his love from me.*

PSALM 66:20 NCV

Nothing can be louder or more intimidating than silence when you are waiting for an answer to your prayers. In the nighttime of the soul, God's silence thunders down at you, rattling your confidence and leaving you wondering if he has abandoned you.

At those times when God is silent, you must place your hope in two mighty truths: the truth of God's sovereignty and the truth of his faithfulness. God answers all your prayers, but always in his own time and in his own way. When you place your hope in him, you will not be disappointed—even when the answer that comes is not what you expected. You are wise to trust him and wait patiently. It is in these times that your faith is tested, strengthened, and established.

The LORD has heard my cry
for help; the LORD will
answer my prayer.

PSALM 6:9 NCV

God, when I do not hear your
voice, help me to rest in your
constant love as I wait for
your answer to my prayer.
Amen.

# THE KITE STRING

*May He grant you according to your heart's desire, And fulfill all your purpose.*

PSALM 20:4 NKJV

A kite is a colorful spectacle as it sails high above the trees. Its reach seems unlimited, its

flight unrestricted as it dips and weaves, glides and bounces with the summer breeze. The kite may seem to be drifting free, but it is not. A taut string, almost invisible against the brightness of the day, keeps it from crashing to the ground or becoming entangled in the branches of a tree.

Your dreams are like the kite. They lift you above the trees and let you soar to new heights. Sometimes your dreams come crashing down because they are not safely anchored to God. When that happens, you must begin again, understanding that allowing God to hold the kite string is what will keep you aloft in a delightful pursuit of your heart's desires.

I stay close to you;
you support me with
your right hand.

PSALM 63:8 NCV


God, hold tight the string that
anchors my heart to yours, for
my hope is ever in you.
Amen.

# GOD SHARES YOUR CARES

*The good man does not escape all troubles—he has them too. But the Lord helps him in each and every one.*

PSALM 34:19 TLB

You face troubles and cares as you journey through life. At times, those cares can over-

whelm you and leave you feeling desperate, alone, and hopeless. You must remember that your hope is in God. When you are struggling to keep your footing, he walks alongside, steadying your feet and helping you to carry your burdens.

Like a gentle shepherd, God guides you around the obstacles that block your path and through the waters that threaten to sweep you off your feet. Sometimes he carries your burdens, and sometimes he carries you. Through it all, you are never alone. He is always with you, sharing your cares, lightening your load, clearing the path before you, and assuring you that you will, one day soon, reach your destination.

It is God who arms me with
strength and makes my way
perfect. He makes my
feet like the feet of a deer;
he enables me to stand
on the heights.

PSALM 18:32–33 NIV

God, thank you for sharing
my cares and walking with
me through all the troubles I
encounter in this life. You are
my hope and my helper.
Amen.

# faith hope

moments of peace in the presence of God

*love*

Those who know
you, LORD, will trust
you; you do not
abandon anyone
who comes to you.

PSALM 9:10 GNT

*faith*

# TRUE NORTH

*Teach me thy way, O LORD; I will walk in thy truth: unite my heart to fear thy name.*

PSALM 86:11 KJV

The strong and unmistakable light of the North Star has been beaming down from the heavens since the dawn of creation. The North Star is beautiful to the casual stargazer, but it holds much more significance for mariners, explorers, travelers, or those who have lost their way. For them, its radiant beam is a practical symbol of hope and safety, pointing the way to true north.

The light of God's love for you is strong and unmistakable. It also beams down on you from the heavens to fill you with hope and to guide you safely to your destination. When you have lost your bearings and don't know which way to turn, the light of God's love illuminates your way. As long as you follow its beam, his constant love will guide you safely home.

Send out your light and your truth; let them guide me. Let them lead me to your holy mountain, to the place where you live.

PSALM 43:3 NLT

I will always keep my eyes on you and faithfully follow after your love, God, for you alone are my true north. Amen.

# THE MASTER PLAN

*Teach me how to live, O LORD.*

PSALM 27:11 NLT

An architect carefully creates a master plan for each new building, plotting all the

details on paper before the first beam of wood is cut or the first nail is driven into place. The integrity of the structure depends on the architect's skill and the degree to which the builders follow the master plan.

God has a master plan for your life as well. When you disregard that plan or deviate from it in significant ways, you create an unstable structure that could come crashing down. When that happens, you must cling to hope and turn to God, the divine architect. He is always ready to help you rebuild your life. If it is too late for master plan A, then your faithful God will unfold the blueprint for master plan B.

I will instruct you and teach
you in the way you should
go; I will counsel you and
watch over you.

PSALM 32:8 NIV

God, I will look to you as the
architect of my life. Help me
build wisely, according to
your master plan.
Amen

# A NEW WAY OF THINKING

*Why art thou cast down, O my soul? And why art thou disquieted in me? hope thou in God: for I shall yet praise him for the help of his countenance.*

PSALM 42:5 KJV

Thoughts of failure, loss, and hopelessness can invade your mind, chasing, tormenting, and even destroying you.  You run from these thoughts, only to find that they are nipping at your heels. You try to hide, only to realize that they are stalking you.

When angry and bitter thoughts leave you running for your life, God offers sanctuary and shelter. With one wave of his mighty hand, he chases away the brutal thoughts, and, one by one, he replaces them with thoughts of kindness, goodness, gentleness, and faith. Love transforms your mind, and hope restores your heart. He promises that even though you may hear the wild beasts growling in the distance, they can never again harm you as long as you dwell in the shelter of his loving arms.

Keep me as the apple of the eye, hide me under the shadow of thy wings.

PSALM 17:8 KJV

God, I thank you for restoring hope to my heart and peace to my mind. You are my Savior and my God. Amen.

# QUESTIONS AND DOUBTS

*Sustain me according to your promise, and I will live; do not let my hopes be dashed.*

PSALM 119:116 NIV

In the utter stillness of a cavern deep underground, a single drop of water falls onto  the surface of a small pond—and then another and another and another. With time, the pond swells until the entire chamber is underwater. Doubt enters your life in the same way—one drop at a time.

When you experience loss or disappointment, it is natural for you to have questions and experience doubt. But you can bring your questions and doubts to God. He will help you resolve your doubts and find the peace you seek. It may take longer than you expect for the answers to come, but they will come. You can know God's true and lasting peace as you allow your doubts to flow out into the river of God's love.

When doubts filled my mind,
your comfort gave me
renewed hope and cheer.

PSALM 94:19 NLT

God, I bring my questions
and doubts to you, and I trust
that you will sustain me, for
my hope is in you.
Amen.

# WHAT REALLY MATTERS

*They that sow in tears shall reap in joy. He that goeth forth and weepeth, bearing precious seed, shall doubtless come again with rejoicing, bringing his sheaves with him.*

PSALM 126:5–6 KJV

Athletes often find it necessary to persevere and go beyond the pain of injury. They continue playing in order to finish the game. They are trained to focus their attention on what really matters in competition—the win.

Loss and disappointment can cause you to lose sight of the things that are truly important in your life. You may want to leave the playing field and nurse your injury on the sideline; you may want to give in to hopelessness and despair. If you let that happen, however, you forget that others are counting on you to stay in the game. You forget that God created you to win. The miraculous love of God can help you see past the pain and find a new level of strength and courage.

God, I must keep my promises
to you. I will give you my
offerings to thank you, because
you have saved me from
death. You have kept me from
being defeated. So I will walk
with God in light among
the living.

PSALM 56:12–13 NCV

God, thank you for helping
me stay in the game and
focus on what really
matters—winning in life!
Amen.

# WONDER AND AWE

*Trust the LORD and his mighty power.*
*Remember his miracles and all his wonders*
*and his fair decisions.*

PSALM 105:4–5 CEV

A newborn child lies sleeping in her mother's arms. She is a gift from God. How can you explain the softness of her skin, the delicateness of her lashes, and the sculpture of her lips?

You cannot. Nor can you explain why God's gifts sometimes seem less than perfect—the little one whose life spans only one day, or the child who must face a lifetime with a disability. Asking why can leave you with overwhelming feelings of disappointment, even anger. But talking to God fills you with hope. He does not always give you the answers you seek, but he does gently remind you that every life—no matter how brief, no matter how challenged—is a miracle. God is always at your side, helping you to see through the tears to the promise.

The LORD is righteous in everything he does; he is filled with kindness. The LORD is close to all who call on him, yes, to all who call on him sincerely.

PSALM 145:17–18 NLT

God, help me to see the miracles in my life through your eyes.
Amen.

# A BRIGHT NEW DAY

*If thou, LORD, shouldst mark iniquities, O LORD, who shall stand? But there is forgiveness with thee, that thou mayest be feared.*

PSALM 130:3–4 KJV

Past failures and disappointments can hover over you like leaden clouds, refusing to yield to the promise of sunlight and clear skies. When you find yourself surrounded by gray thoughts and gray feelings, it may seem difficult to dream of happier times. But there is great hope. When you find yourself in such a situation, God is there to help.

When you call out to him, he extends his hand to you and leads you out from under the foreboding clouds of the past and into the light of a new day. He offers hope for a new beginning. The journey into the sunlight is usually not an easy one, but God will walk with you every step of the way. A new life lies before you.

The salvation of the righteous is from the LORD;
he is their refuge in the
time of trouble.

PSALM 37:39 NRSV

God, I will place my hope in
you as you walk together
from beneath the dark clouds
of the past and into the
promise of the future.
Amen.

# SIMPLY BELIEVE

*I believe that I shall see the goodness of the LORD in the land of the living.*

PSALM 27:13 NRSV

Every fall as the cold winds of winter approach, flocks of birds fly southward to

warm climes and mild breezes. With no map to guide them, they fly confidently, accepting instinctively that their winter refuges wait at the end of their journey.

There are times in your life when you must fly south symbolically, away from the winter winds of despair and hopelessness. As you take flight, God will provide a refuge for your troubled soul in his goodness, mercy, kindness, and compassion. He asks you to believe that he will provide gentle breezes for your journey. He asks you to believe that his never-failing love will go with you wherever your journey takes you. Simply believe, he tells you as you lean into the wind and surrender yourself to healing and hope.

Our fathers trusted in You;
They trusted, and You
delivered them. They cried
to You, and were delivered;
They trusted in You, and
were not ashamed.

PSALM 22:4–5 NKJV

God, my future is in
your hands.
Amen.

# WINNING OVER WORRY

*Our LORD, we belong to you. We tell you what worries us, and you won't let us fall.*

PSALM 55:22 CEV

Worry is really fear dressed in sheep's clothing. Disguised as a friend, it betrays you

when you are most vulnerable, bringing before you images of what has been and images of what might be in its quest to steal your present and sabotage your future. Worry is a formidable threat to the tranquility of your soul.

You can win over worry by seeing it for what it is—a thief that can destroy your peace and steal your hope. When you turn to God and submit your anxious thoughts to him, he can replace them with pure and praiseworthy thoughts, thoughts that will help build your future, thoughts that will restore your joy of living. Fear, stripped of its flimsy disguise, is then left to slink back into the shadows.

The LORD is my light and my salvation; whom shall I fear? The LORD is the strength of my life; of whom shall I be afraid?

PSALM 27:1–2 KJV

God, thank you for filling my mind with good thoughts so that I can win my battle against worry and fear. Amen.

# THE WORK OF WAITING

*Wait for the LORD; Be strong, and let your heart take courage; Yes, wait for the LORD.*

PSALM 27:14 NASB

A strong and confident retriever strains against its leash, willing itself to be still. Every

muscle twitches with expectation as it waits for its master's command. Like this magnificent animal, you often find waiting to be hard.

God knows that it is not easy for you to obey him as you strain against your natural instincts; nevertheless, at times he asks you to wait. He also knows that when you wait on him, you grow in faith and learn to respond with strength and wisdom. Those times give you the opportunity to place your hope in God's faithfulness rather than to focus on your own need for gratification. When you face difficult times and find yourself waiting for God to answer your prayers, you are preparing yourself to receive his perfect answer.

Be still before the LORD, and
wait patiently for him; do not
fret over those who prosper
in their way, over those who
carry out evil devices.

PSALM 37:7 NRSV

God, when you ask me to
wait, I will obey and place
my hope in your great love
and faithfulness.
Amen.

# PAUSING FOR POWER

*You are awesome, O God, in your sanctuary; the*
*God of Israel gives power and strength to his people.*
PSALM 68:35 NIV

Tragedy and loss can leave
you feeling powerless, like a single flower that the wind whips
and breaks. You may feel that you
no longer have control over the
circumstances of your life, and
you may feel hopeless and alone.
In the midst of those difficult
times, you may feel that God is
far away.

But God promises that he will always be
with you. Even when anger and grief cause
you to lose a sense of his presence, he is closer
than the beating of your own heart. He assures
you that no tragedy can separate you from his
amazing love. And he allows you to draw
from his power to take responsibility for your
life again, to see past your heartache, and to
find hope and healing in his presence.

I can lie down and go to
sleep, and I will wake up
again, because the LORD
gives me strength.

PSALM 3:5 NCV

Gracious God, thank you for
loving me, even in the midst of
my anger and grief, and thank
you for giving me the power
and strength to live again.
Amen.

# TAKING HOLD OF GRACE

*Grace is poured into thy lips: therefore God hath blessed thee for ever.*

PSALM 45:2 KJV

God's grace is abundantly evident in the world around you. The rosy blush of the sunrise as it bursts above the horizon reminds you that the sparkling dawn of a brand-new day is replacing the long dark night. The resplendent spectrum of the rainbow reminds you that the sun is busy chasing away the rain clouds. The whimsical laugh of a child at play reminds you that you, too, are a child—God's child.

God's grace is evident in his creation, and it is God's gift to help you through the difficult times that life often brings your way. God's grace is the visible evidence of his everlasting love. Even when it appears that sorrow and grief threaten your joy, God offers his grace to you and you experience the hope of his promise.

O sing to the LORD a new song, for he has done marvelous things. His right hand and his holy arm have gotten him victory.

PSALM 98:1 NRSV

God, when my heart is heavy with sorrow, your grace lifts me up and gives me a new song to sing.
Amen.

# RETURNING TO LIFE

*You will show me the way of life, granting me the joy of your presence and the pleasures of living with you forever.*

PSALM 16:11 NLT

So far is the planet Pluto from the sun that it takes 248.5 years for Pluto to make its way around the outskirts of the solar system. An observer on Pluto would view the sun as little more than a relatively bright star, with little ability to warm or illuminate the planet's icy consistency of frozen gas and metallic stone.

You may feel at times that your heart has taken on the characteristics of a faraway planet. But no matter how you might feel, God promises that nothing can separate you from him and his great love for you. When you place your hope in him, you can count on him to pull you back into a healing and life-sustaining orbit, where the rays of his presence will warm you and illuminate your dark places.

I have said, Mercy shall be built up for ever: thy faithfulness shalt thou establish in the very heavens.

PSALM 89:2 KJV

God, in the darkest hours of my life, I will place my hope in your faithful love for me. Amen.

# MORE THAN ENOUGH

*Many, O LORD my God, are thy wonderful works which thou hast done, and thy thoughts which are to us-ward: they cannot be reckoned up in order unto thee: if I would declare and speak of them, they are more than can be numbered.*

PSALM 40:5 KJV

A small boy stands in the sunshine, puffing in the direction of a dandelion. When his boyish bluster reaches its target, the fluffy seeds float through the air to the music of the small boy's laughter. To the boy, this is a magical game, but to the flower, it is simple reproduction. There will soon be new dandelions popping up everywhere.

Troubles can multiply even more quickly than the sturdy, determined seeds of the dandelion flower. Whether you blow them into the air yourself or they simply fly on the wings of the wind, troubles can quickly overwhelm your life. The good news is that God's thoughts are constantly on you, and he can help you deal with each one. He is more than enough to help you weed out the troubles in your life.

You chart the path ahead of me and tell me where to stop and rest. Every moment you know where I am.

PSALM 139:3 NLT

Thank you, God, for your loving, watchful care over my life. I release my troubles to you, for I know that you are more than enough to handle them.

Amen.

faith hope

moments of peace in the presence of God

*love*

*patience*

*In the morning, O
LORD, you hear my
voice; in the morning
I lay my requests
before you and wait
in expectation.*
PSALM 5:3 NIV

# DESERT STREAMS

*He turns a desert into pools of water, a parched land into springs of water.*

PSALM 107:35 NRSV

On your journey, you sometimes pass through desert areas filled with nothing but uninviting cacti and sun-scorched sands as far as the eye can see—seemingly barren wastelands on the landscape of your life. What you do not see so easily is that the desert is teaming with robust life. Underground streams support a variety of hearty vegetation and lively creatures. God has not lessened the intensity of the sun's rays for their benefit. The sun shines on, but God has equipped the desert's flora and fauna to withstand the extremities of their home.

You pass through dry, parched areas in your journey through life. When you do, you must remember that God will faithfully provide for you, just as he has for the plants and creatures of the desert.

O God, thou art my God; early
will I seek thee: my soul
thirsteth for thee, my flesh
longeth for thee in a dry and
thirsty land, where no water is.

PSALM 63:1 KJV

God, when I need streams in
the deserts of my life, I will
place my hope in your faithfulness and love for me.
Amen.

# THE COST OF COMMITMENT

*Commit everything you do to the Lord. Trust him to help you do it and he will.*

PSALM 37:5 TLB

Nestled snugly among the branches of a gnarled blackjack oak, a bright red cardinal and its mate carefully guard a

nest full of eggs. Ever watchful, the adult birds vigorously defend the nest against all sorts of predators. Until the eggs are hatched and the baby cardinals are mature enough to survive on their own, the adults are fully committed to their care.

God is even more committed to you than those amazing cardinals are to their little brood. When you are heartbroken and vulnerable, God is there to defend, sustain, and heal you in preparation for the day when you can fly high and strong on the currents of life. When you place your hope and trust in his faithfulness, you will not be disappointed. He is committed to your care.

God, your love is so precious!
You protect people in the
shadow of your wings.

PSALM 36:7 NCV

God, when I feel weak and
helpless, I will put my hope
and trust in your commitment
to guard my life and nurse me
back to health and wholeness.
Amen.

# THE EYES OF UNDERSTANDING

*Thy hands have made me and fashioned me:*
*give me understanding, that I may learn thy*
*commandments.*

PSALM 119:73 KJV

The sunset is one of God's magnificent wonders. Sweeping across the horizon as if painted by God's own hand, it imbues the receding sunlight with indescribable splendor and signals that one day is giving way to another—a celestial changing of the guard.

Your life is full of days as well, but you seldom pass as smoothly from one to the other. You fail to view the sunsets in your life in the same way you do the sunrises. Endings can be just as beautiful as beginnings if you allow God to open the eyes of your understanding. When you truly realize the miracle of the sunset, you will no longer cling to the remains of the day. You will instead revel in its beauty, celebrating life to its fullest.

In ages past you laid the
foundation of the earth, and
the heavens are the work
of your hands.

PSALM 102:25 NLT

Great Creator, open the eyes of
my understanding to appreciate
the sunsets in my life.
Amen.

# DIVINE DESTINY

*The LORD will work out his plans for my life—*
*for your faithful love, O LORD, endures forever.*
PSALM 138:8 NLT

Whipped by the wind, the hungry flames of a wildfire devour everything in sight; the orange-red glow illuminates the night sky. The morning light reveals the devastation in its aftermath. A sumptuous green forest has given way to rows of blackened stumps and a smoky expanse of charred ground. Yet God renews even the blackened forest. In a few months, new growth springs forth from the charred ground, and flowers and vegetation soon cover the ground like a warm, inviting blanket.

At times, you may feel that a raging wildfire has swept unchecked across your life and left the rich colorful texture of your existence smudged and stunted. Even then you can rejoice, for God can also give new life to you. All he asks is that you place your hope in him.

Like trees planted in the
Temple of the LORD, they
will grow strong in the court-
yards of our God.

PSALM 92:13 NCV

God, thank you for your
promise of life and renewal.
Amen.

# A WEALTH OF WISDOM

*The fear of the LORD is the beginning of wisdom; all who follow his precepts have good understanding. To him belongs eternal praise.*

PSALM 111:10 NIV

Turbulence churns overhead as the distraught ocean whips against the ship. The captain struggles to find safe harbor. The captain knows that under such trying circumstances it is easy to become disoriented and be swept into treacherously shallow water where the vessel could be torn apart on the rocks. Rather than trust his own senses, the wise captain checks his compass and watches carefully to spot the guiding beam from the lighthouse.

Similarly, you can become disoriented as you make your way through life's stormy seas. God promises that he will guide you with his wisdom and will light the troubled waters with the faithful beams of his love. When you place your hope in him, you can be sure that you will find your way safely home.

Take me out of the net
that is hidden for me,
for you are my refuge.

PSALM 31:4 NRSV

Mighty God, thank you for
the wisdom you provide as I
navigate the stormy seas of
my life. Thank you for the
light of your love that guides
me safely into harbor.
Amen.

# MYSTERIOUS WAYS

*I do not concern myself with great matters or things too wonderful for me. But I have stilled and quieted my soul; like a weaned child with its mother.*

PSALM 131:1–2 NIV

The sky darkens and ominous clouds form a wall from the ground upward as far as the eye can see. From its midst, a deafening roar and a swirling funnel emerge. Wind and dust and debris fill the air as the tornado cuts a destructive swath across the landscape. There are amazing exceptions. Amid the debris of one home, a solitary wall still stands. On it hangs a knickknack shelf, which holds a fragile teapot, cup, and saucer—all mysteriously untouched by the storm's fury.

Even when devastating storms cut their terrible paths across your life, the peace and love that God puts within you cannot be touched. He will never leave you, and he will give you the strength and the courage to rebuild your life and look with hope into a bright future.

The LORD is gracious, and full of compassion; slow to anger, and of great mercy.

PSALM 145:8 KJV

God, your mysterious ways give me love, peace, and hope in the midst of life's most powerful storms.
Amen.

# FACING THE FUTURE

*When anxiety was great within me, your consolation brought joy to my soul.*

PSALM 94:19 NIV

A giant tortoise lumbers contentedly along on its way to nowhere, stopping often to

nibble on the grass. A loud noise pierces the air, and a shadow crosses the tortoise's path. The tortoise stops right where it is, pulls its head into its shell, and shuts out the world.

You may experience times when you wish you could pull inside yourself to avoid emotional pain, fear, or disappointment. Brief periods of solitude can often help you process your thoughts and gain inner strength. It would be tempting to stay there. However, just as the tortoise would soon starve if it remained in its shell indefinitely, so, too, would you starve emotionally if you remained walled up within yourself. God can help you face your circumstances and walk forward with confidence and hope.

Create in me a clean heart, O
God; and renew a right
spirit within me.

PSALM 51:10 KJV

Gracious God, thank you for
drawing me out of my fearful, anxious shell and into the
light of your love. Thank you
for new promise and purpose
for my life.
Amen.

# RISING TO THE CHALLENGE

*Be of good courage, And He shall strengthen your heart, All you who hope in the LORD.*

PSALM 31:24 NKJV

A stony peak rises in the distance—cold and formidable against the early morning sky. To the casual observer, it would seem to be an unforgiving fortress, off limits to any human. Then a climber is spotted scaling the face of the peak, inching upward—one toehold, one handhold at a time.

When you look ahead and see nothing but cold, stony, uninviting peaks crowding the landscape of your life, you must not lose heart. God has promised to help you tackle every challenge, and he will give you hope and encouragement to continue upward one toehold and one handhold at a time. God will hold you steady as you make your way to the summit. He will restore your hope as you gaze down into the lush valley on the other side.

Yes, he alone is my Rock, my
rescuer, defense and fortress.
Why then should I be tense
with fear when troubles come?

PSALM 62:2 TLB

God, when my future seems to
be filled with stony peaks, I
will place my hope in your
strength and faithfulness.
Amen.

# SONGS FOR THE SOUL

*Through each night I sing his songs, praying to God who gives me life.*

PSALM 42:8 NLT

Atop the fence post, a robin lifts its head toward heaven and its voice in song. Other troubadours take up the chorus, and a jubilee of birdsong fills the air, refreshing the heart of their Creator. Why does the robin sing? It sings because it must; a song is its voice. The robin's song was designed to bring constant praise to God.

Like the robin, you are God's creation. Unlike the robin, however, you have been given a greater gift. You have been given a will. When you lift your voice to God, it is because you choose to do so. Your songs of praise delight the heart of God. Your songs bring comfort, solace, and refreshment to your own life as well, strengthening you in difficult times.

Clap your hands, all you peoples; shout to God with loud songs of joy. For the LORD, the Most High, is awesome, a great king over all the earth.

PSALM 47:1–2 NRSV

Teach me to sing your praises during good times and bad times, God. Strengthen, comfort, and heal me as I lift my voice in song. Amen.

# ICE STORMS

*Thou hast turned for me my mourning into dancing: thou hast put off my sackcloth, and girded me with gladness; To the end that my glory may sing praise to thee, and not be silent. O LORD my God, I will give thanks unto thee for ever.*

PSALM 30:11–12 KJV

Icicles hang from the eaves of houses and the branches of trees. They are visible testaments that cold winds and freezing temperatures followed the rain too closely. The morning and afternoon rays of the sun beat down upon them in an effort to melt them away drop by drop.

The bitter winds of calamity blow across your life; sometimes they follow too soon on the heels of other losses and disappointments. Your tears turn to ice. Ruinous troubles and afflictions weigh you down. Your emotions are locked in their cold grip. But it doesn't matter, because even then God is able to reach you with the sunlight of his love, melting away your frozen places. As long as you place your hope in him, no icy prison can hold you.

Whoever is wise, let him heed
these things and consider the
great love of the LORD.

PSALM 107:43 NIV

God, when my heart seems to
be locked in sorrow's icy grip,
I will look to you for help and
place my hope in the sunlight
of your love.
Amen.

# LEAPING FOR JOY

*The LORD is my strength and my shield; in him my heart trusts; so I am helped, and my heart exults, and with my song I give thanks to him.*

PSALM 28:7 NRSV

Not far offshore, a pod of whales moves smoothly through the water on the way to warmer seas. As the whales pass, the magnificent creatures take turns breaching, thrusting their huge bodies high into the air before splashing on their bellies or their backs. Those who study whales now believe they breach for only one reason—they want to. Perhaps they enjoy the way the sun feels on their skin; perhaps they enjoy the rush of air. Whatever the case, it appears that whales leap from the water for the sheer joy it brings them.

No matter what your circumstances might be, you, too, can leap for joy, reminding yourself that God has given you many blessings—the unfailing miracles of his love, his peace, and his promise that he will always be with you.

Let me go to the altar of
God, to God my highest joy,
and I will give thanks to you
on the lyre, O God, my God.

PSALM 43:4 GOD'S WORD

Loving God, thank you for
the blessings you have placed
in my life—blessings so
wonderful that they
cause me to leap for joy.
Amen.

# AUTUMN LEAVES

*Show me, O LORD, my life's end and the*
*number of my days; let me know how fleeting*
*is my life.*

The leaves of autumn—burnished gold, dusty red, muted orange, and bright yellow—float through the air and cover the ground, a glorious tribute to what was and soon will be no more. Does it seem strange that God would invest such exquisite beauty in a season of dying? Consider this, that unless you are willing to celebrate the end of what you know, you will not enter into what is yet to be.

It doesn't matter what you are facing, whether the end of your physical life, the end of a lifelong dream, or the end of your youth. Look at the beauty in the leaves of autumn and trust God for what lies ahead, including the glory of heaven. God will never disappoint you when you place your hope in him.

I have been young, and now
am old, yet I have not seen
the righteous forsaken or
their children begging bread.

PSALM 37:25 NRSV

All-knowing God, help me
to appreciate the beauty of
autumn leaves as I walk with
you into the future.
Amen.

# STAYING STEADY THROUGH TOUGH TIMES

*As for me, I will always have hope; I will praise you more and more.*

PSALM 71:14 NIV

The tendrils of ivy climb the sides of the brick structure until they cover every square

inch. Ivy stems are strong, hearty, and almost unbreakable, and they grip the surface so tightly that only the most determined effort can dislodge them. Ivy is capable of weathering the extremes of both heat and cold without withering and falling away.

When you place your hope in God, you are clinging to him in the same tenacious way that ivy clings to brick and mortar. When the sun is warm and the rain is gentle, you grow strong and hearty, reaching and moving as you strengthen your grip on God's never-failing love. Then when the strong winds blow and the rain beats at you, you know that you can hang on. You cannot be moved.

Happy is he that hath the
God of Jacob for his help,
whose hope is in
the LORD his God.

PSALM 146:5 KJV

Mighty God, help me to cling to
you like ivy clings to the brick.
Amen.

# GOD IS ON THE THRONE

*The LORD is in His holy temple; the LORD's throne is in heaven; His eyes behold, His eyelids test the sons of men.*

PSALM 11:4 NASB

A tiny child lies in her crib, smiling broadly as her mother coos from just above the railing. The moment her mother steps out of sight, the child's sweet smile disappears. She begins to whimper. Because she can no longer see her mother or sense her presence, the child believes she has been abandoned.

As you begin to put your hope in God, you are in many respects like a small child. When you experience difficult times and do not immediately sense his presence, you may feel that he has left you and no longer cares about you. As you grow in your faith, you realize that there is more to God than what you can see and understand. His eyes of love never leave you. His hand is always there.

*A*s for me, my prayer is to
you, O LORD. At an
acceptable time, O God, in
the abundance of your
steadfast love, answer me.

PSALM 69:13 NRSV

*G*od, help me as I grow in
hope and faith.
Amen.

faith hope

moments of peace in the presence of God

*love*

*How wonderful are
the good things
you keep for those
who honor you!
Everyone knows how
good you are,
how securely you
protect those
who trust you.*
PSALM 31:19 GNT

*abundance*

# A PATTERN OF PATIENCE

*I waited patiently for the LORD; he inclined to me and heard my cry.*

PSALM 40:1 NRSV

Tulips and daffodils, in all the brilliant colors of spring, hide throughout the long winter in tight little shells deep beneath the surface of the soil. You barely know they exist as the wind blows and the cold holds you in its grip. But with the first warming breeze of spring, you notice green shoots bursting through the surface of the soil. Soon waving everywhere are the red, pink, and yellow flags that represent God's faithful promise that summer and winter, springtime and harvest will continue on the earth, and in your life, each at its appointed time.

You must be patient and cling to your hope in God. In his perfect time, the ambassadors of spring will burst forth in your life once more, fulfilling the promise of God's faithfulness to his creation.

You made me suffer a lot, but you will bring me back from this deep pit and give me new life. You will make me truly great and take my sorrow away.

PSALM 71:20–21 CEV

God, thank you for the promise of springtime in my life. I will wait patiently through the difficult seasons and hope earnestly in your faithfulness. Amen.

# WINGS OF MERCY

*O taste and see that the LORD is good: blessed is the man that trusteth in him.*

PSALM 34:8 KJV

High above the treetops, a black-winged hawk soars majestically. The bird's swoops

and glides appear effortless as it moves along on the late afternoon breezes. It seems to fear nothing above or below as it sails back and forth, up and down, soaking up the last lingering rays of the sun. Its awesome grace is breathtaking.

In the midst of difficult times, it's tempting to look up at the hawk and wish that you, too, could sail along on gentle breezes, high above your painful circumstances. During those seasons when your strength seems almost gone, be assured that God is beside you, ready to sweep you up onto his mighty wings of mercy and grace. There you find rest, comfort, and healing for your broken hearts and wounded spirits.

You have not handed me
over to my enemies but have
set me in a safe place.

PSALM 31:8 NCV

God, when my life seems unbearably
painful, I will place my hope in you. I
will forsake my own failing strength
and rest on your wings of mercy.
Amen.

# SURE FOOTING

*Let everyone bless God and sing his praises; for he holds our lives in his hands, and he holds our feet to the path.*

PSALM 66:8–9 TLB

So steep and treacherous are the paths along the walls of the Grand Canyon that those who wish to traverse them rarely set out on foot. They depend on remarkable animals with hoofs designed to hug the narrow, dusty paths and bodies proportioned for maximum strength, endurance, and balance.

In the course of your life, many of you will encounter certain mountain paths that are simply too difficult and dangerous for you to attempt alone. You feel that your feet are unsteady and uncertain; you are ill-equipped mentally and physically. But when you set out on those trails, you can depend on God to keep you from falling. He will provide the assistance you need to secure your footing and to carry your burdens safely to the top of the canyon wall.

He will command his angels
concerning you to guard you
in all your ways; they will lift
you up in their hands, so that
you will not strike your foot
against a stone.

PSALM 91:11–12 NIV

Faithful God, when I must
follow a steep and treacherous
path on my journey through
life, I will place my hope and
trust in your promise to
help me reach my
destination safely.
Amen.

# THE SOURCE OF HOPE

*Now, Lord, what wait I for? my hope is in thee.*
PSALM 39:7 KJV

The song of the robin, the majesty of snow-covered mountain peaks, the lustrous  beauty of a spring flower, and the predictable movement of the stars in the night sky are but a few of the wonders that point you to God, the source of all hope. They are reminders that no circumstance—poverty, pain, sickness, loss, disappointment, grief, even the prospect of your own death—can steal your hope when it is safely anchored in God.

God is the author of all hope, and he will never leave your side as you walk through the dark, confusing, lonely, and painful places in your life. He will replace your clouds of despair with the brilliant, penetrating light of his everlasting love. He will fill your heart with peace and your mind with wisdom and understanding.

Shout with joy to the LORD,
O earth! Worship the LORD
with gladness. Come before
him, singing with joy.

PSALM 100:1–2 NLT

Thank you, God, for a voice
with which to sing your
praises with my whole heart.
Amen.

# GOD'S FAITHFULNESS

*All those who know your mercy, Lord, will count on you for help. For you have never yet forsaken those who trust in you.*

PSALM 9:10 TLB

The vows and promises you exchange with those you love provide you with a strong foundation on which to build your life. Your word is your bond and your commitment. The faithfulness you give, as well as the faithfulness you receive, fills you with confidence and comforts you in your times of need. But the faithfulness of your closest family and friends appears as a pale shadow next to the splendor of God's faithfulness.

God is faithful to you no matter what. He gives you his full attention when you reach out for his love, assurance, and support. God never breaks his promises. And he is always there for you. By believing this and affirming it often, you take on a measure of his strength and reflect his goodness to others.

The LORD is my rock and my fortress and my deliverer; My God, my strength, in whom I will trust; My shield and the horn of my salvation, my stronghold.

PSALM 18:2 NKJV

God, let me walk this earth with confidence. Help me always to trust in your faithful love, guidance, and protection. Amen.

# SEEKING AND YEARNING FOR GOD

*Hear my cry, O God; listen to my prayer. From the end of the earth I call to you, when my heart is faint.*

PSALM 61:1–2 NRSV

Until you place your life fully in God's hands, you will never quiet the anxious thoughts that can cry out from within and leave you feeling unhappy and defeated. You can search frantically for happiness, success, and fulfillment. You can flail about and wonder why you are never satisfied, why you are always restless. You may wonder why new acquisitions merely whet your desire for more.

What you are yearning for and trying to find has been there all the time. God alone can satisfy your desperate longings. Without him, even the sources of human happiness, such as family and possessions, invite stress and agitation. Only when you make God the center of your life will you find true fulfillment.

*I* cry to God Most High, to God
who fulfills his purpose for me.

PSALM 57:2 NRSV

*G*od, as I look to you, fill my
life to overflowing with your
peace and joy. Keep me always
in the palm of your hand.
Amen.

# GOD'S JOY AND DELIGHT IN YOUR LIFE

*The LORD is kind and shows mercy, He does not become angry quickly but is full of love. The LORD is good to everyone; he is merciful to all he has made.*

PSALM 145:8–9 NCV

When you think of those you love—family and friends, mentors and heroes—joy and affection fill your heart. Because they are in the world, your life is brighter and more meaningful. You watch for opportunities to show them how much you care for them and value them. You jump at chances to nourish and to sustain them, to cheer them and to make their hearts glad. Their very existence is a cause for celebration. When they are happy, you are happy.

As children of God, you mimic him in these feelings for your loved ones, feelings that are dim reflections of his profound delight in you as his children. He wants to see you happy and fulfilled, and he wants you to know he is the source of the abundant blessings in your life.

The Lord himself is my inheritance, my prize. He is my food and drink, my highest joy!

PSALM 16:5 TLB

Knowing that I am your child brings me great joy and delight, God. Help me to be happy and to achieve all that I was created to do.

Amen.

# COMFORT IN GOD

*I have set the LORD always before me: because he is at my right hand, I shall not be moved.*

PSALM 16:8 KJV

You live with a daily onslaught of tragic news from around the world and close to

home—sad images from the television, heartbreaking stories from a dear friend. These hard realities can rob you of your joy and replace it with fear.

You must constantly bolster your hope in the eternal love and protection of God, who guides you always. His power touches your heart, mind, and soul. This mystery of God's daily work in your life is beyond your ability to understand. It is the great mystery of life that you are, as a child of God and a tabernacle of his Spirit, mighty and invincible. You can lay your fears to rest. You can give God your cares and burdens and place your trust completely in him.

You have turned for me my mourning into dancing; You have put off my sackcloth and clothed me with gladness, To the end that my glory may sing praise to You and not be silent.

PSALM 30:11–12 NKJV

God, all I have and all I am comes from you. I place myself wholly in your will and know you will care for me and quiet my fears. Amen.

# LOVING GOD

*I love you, LORD; you are my strength.*

PSALM 18:1 NLT

God's grandeur inspires awe. His perfect goodness is imponderable. He is so big; you  are so small. He is beyond your understanding. How then can you love him? By embracing him and making him part of your daily life.

To do that, you must first acknowledge your utter dependence on him. You must gaze at the world around you with new eyes, eyes full of love and admiration for his countless wonders. You must constantly remind yourself that his handiwork is everywhere and in everything, and that he is greater than the most marvelous thing you can imagine. You must wake up to the truth that you are important because he made you, he loves you, he protects you, and he preserves you. He is your strength.

Let all those who seek You
rejoice and be glad in You; Let
such as love Your salvation
say continually, "The LORD
be magnified!"

PSALM 40:16 NKJV

God, help me to end each day
by whispering an *amen* to you
as I go to sleep and to wake up
each morning with a *hallelujah*
in my heart.
Amen.

# GOD'S MERCY AND COMPASSION

*The LORD is kind and does what is right;*
*your God is merciful.*

PSALM 116:5 NCV

God's mercy and compassion make life bearable and invest it with meaning. You pray

to him for aid, and he answers you. You ask him, the God of light, to protect you, and he does just that. You implore him for wisdom and guidance, and he gives it freely. His deep and abiding concern

for you as his children is manifest in the steadfast love he shows you.

How comforting it is to rest in God's mercy—to know without any doubt that no matter where you fail, no matter where you might be fearful, his mercy abounds. It never ends. It is infinite. How reassuring it is to know that he feels compassion for you and intervenes in your everyday life, with the blessings of his divine mercy.

The LORD is like a father to
his children, tender and
compassionate to
those who fear him.

PSALM 103:13 NLT

God, thank you for your mercy
that is poured out on me. Teach
me to reach out to others as you
have reached out to me.
Amen.

# GOD'S POWER, PRESENCE, AND PEACE

*He will give his people strength. He will bless them with peace.*

PSALM 29:11 TLB

Consider the moments you have when you sense God's power, presence, and peace—

moments when the clouds part and a sudden, all-prevailing sense of peace washes over you. You know then that you are truly loved by almighty God, and you are filled with gratitude and a new sense of

security. It is as if you have suddenly discovered who you really are, and you feel more alive than ever.

These moments become more frequent if you cultivate quality time with God. This requires spiritual discipline and fortitude. If you determine to pursue this course, however, the rewards are boundless and will immeasurably enrich your life. Daily prayer, Scripture reading, and meditation on God's attributes will deepen your understanding and make you a ready receptacle for his grace.

The LORD is my light and the one who saves me. I fear no one. The LORD protects my life; I am afraid of no one.

PSALM 27:1 NCV

God, I don't want to wait until I get to heaven to enjoy your power, your presence, and your peace. Help me receive all that you have for me each day.
Amen.

# GOD'S GREATNESS AND MAJESTY

*My whole being, praise the LORD. LORD my God, you are very great.*

PSALM 104:1–2 NCV

The best way to appreciate the grandeur and glory of God is to shed your weariness and worldly wisdom and begin to see things through childlike eyes. Doing so returns to you your sense of wonder and awe. Christ said as much when he encouraged you to become as a little child, awed by life, but trusting nonetheless in God.

God's greatness and majesty are evidenced everywhere, if you look at the world with childlike eyes—birds fly from branch to branch, fishes swim in the sea, geckos skitter across warm rocks, wolves bay at the moon, and stars shoot across the night sky. A child has no difficulty believing that God made all these things, that he created them all. When you become as a child, you will have no difficulty either.

158

O Lord my God, many and
many a time you have done
great miracles for us, and we
are ever in your thoughts.
Who else can do such glorious things? No one else can
be compared with you.

PSALM 40:5 TLB

God, help me never to
become so grown up that I no
longer revel in the glory of
your creation or accept your
unconditional love for me.
Amen.

# GOD LISTENS TO YOUR PRAYERS

*Through each night I sing his songs, praying to God who gives me life.*

PSALM 42:8 NLT

Pulled between the demands of work and family, you have little opportunity for quiet time. The moments when you can experience God without distraction and interruption are few and precious. The faces of your loved ones are never far from your mind, reminding, cajoling, and requesting.

Yet no matter how fragmented and abbreviated your prayers may become as a result, you can be sure God hears them—not only in those rare moments of peace but also during the frantic hours of activity. He hears you clearly, no matter how mumbled and inarticulate your message may seem. And he is quick to give you the right words to say, the proper response to a crisis, and the kindness and diplomacy you need to navigate your complex and difficult days.

Morning, noon, and night
you hear my concerns and
my complaints.

PSALM 55:17 CEV

God, I bring all my cares to
you. Thank you for listening
and answering me.
Amen.

# PRAYER BANISHES WORRY AND FEAR

*Hear my voice, O God, in my meditation;*
*Preserve my life from fear of the enemy.*

PSALM 64:1 NKJV

Worry and fear are the bane of human existence. Any number of events or circum-

stances can trigger them to cripple or incapacitate you. Worry and fear strike when you feel far from God. They rise up and crash over you when you are not paying attention to what is really important in life—your relationship with God. That's when you need to stay focused.

The more you pray, the closer you draw to God and the better you know him. And the more you pray, the more his presence and power surround you, lifting you up and dissolving your worries and fears. You can cope with whatever comes along because you know you are shored up and strengthened with what he has promised you. You have become a recipient of his bountiful grace.

I cry out to God Most High, to
the God who does everything for
me. He sends help from heaven
and saves me. He punishes those
who chase me. God sends me
his love and truth.

PSALM 57:2–3 NCV

God, I know that you will ban-
ish my fears as I put my trust in
you and walk with you
in prayer.
Amen.

faith hope

moments of peace in the presence of God

*love*

At all times they give
freely and lend to
others, and their
children are a blessing.

PSALM 37:26 GNT

*giving*

# PRAYER HELPS YOU MAKE DECISIONS

*With my whole heart have I sought thee: O let me not wander from thy commandments.*

PSALM 119:10 KJV

Throughout the days of your life, you are presented with moral choices to make. And those choices are not often simple issues of all right and all wrong. Indeed the most difficult situations you face have to do with choosing from a variety of possibilities, with varying shades of good and bad.

Fortunately, you do not have to deal with difficult choices alone and unaided. If you ask God, he will enlighten you. He will show you the way to go. He has already given you his commandments to light your way through the maze of facts and emotions. And he waits patiently for you to bring each one before him. He will help you do what is right for your life and the lives of those you love.

Thy word have I hid in mine heart, that I might not sin against thee.

PSALM 119:11 KJV

God, thank you for the direction you give and the way you fill my heart with quiet assurance.
Amen.

# THE LORD WANTS TO USE YOUR TALENTS

*Let the beauty of the LORD our God be upon us,*
*And establish the work of our hands for us;*
*Yes, establish the work of our hands.*

PSALM 90:17 NKJV

Each one of you is unique and irreplaceable in the eyes of God. And you have been given talents and abilities that are yours alone. The key to achieving satisfaction and success with your talents is to place them always at the service of God. You should ask for his direction and pray for his guidance so you may use your gifts fruitfully and fully in his eyes.

God has a plan for you, and he has equipped you for your journey. Your responsibility is to seek his will for you and to allow him to perfect and refine your talents and abilities until they are functioning as God intended them to function. It is then that you can be sure he will bless the work of your hands.

You are their glorious
strength. Our power is based
on your favor.

PSALM 89:17 NLT

God, I give all my talents and
abilities to you. Help me to grow
in my determination to be all
that you have created me to be.
Amen.

# FAITH, HOPE, AND LOVE

*Yes, Lord, let your constant love surround us, for our hopes are in you alone.*

PSALM 33:22 TLB

The spiritual strength that God gives you is founded on the wonder-working triad of faith, hope, and love. Your Lord shows you how you are to behave with others by actively demonstrating these three virtues through his own unblemished behavior toward you.

If you take God at his word, your ordinary day-to-day life should be a reflection or an acting-out of his promises to you; and your relationships with others should be an energetic, vital mirror image of the trustworthy, loving, and merciful God you have come to know. It is really as simple as one, two, three. Faith, hope, love. You must strive for faith, hope, and love in all your dealings, whether with others or with yourself, if you want to be fully pleasing to God.

Be of good courage, and he
shall strengthen your heart,
all ye that hope in the LORD.

PSALM 31:24 KJV

God, I want to build my life
upon the principles of faith,
hope, and love. Guide me and
keep me on the right path.
Amen.

# GOD IS IN THE DETAILS

*I will meditate about your glory, splendor, majesty, and miracles.*

PSALM 145:5 TLB

God is evident in a tear or in a far-off whistle. He is in the twinkle of a stranger's eye and in a certain shade of blue. He is in the warmth of a handshake and in the missing front teeth of a five-year-old. He is between the lines of handwritten letters and in the nervous laughter of teenage girls. He is in the invisible arc made by a hawk on a fine autumn day. He is the energy you use to write your to-do lists, and he is in the itch to take a break in the middle of the day.

God surrounds you with reminders of his presence. He is in kept promises and acts of love and mercy. God is in every sigh, whisper, and exclamation. God is by you now.

This is the LORD's doing; it is
marvelous in our eyes. This is
the day that the LORD has
made; let us rejoice
and be glad in it.

PSALM 118:23–24 NRSV

God, thank you for your
presence in my life. Give me
eyes to see the many things
you do for me.

Amen.

# THE KINGDOM OF GOD IS NOW

*Your kingdom is an everlasting kingdom, and your dominion endures throughout all generations.*

PSALM 145:13 NRSV

Heaven is usually spoken of as a faraway place that you reach only at the end of a godly life. But God's reign over all that he created is right here in the present day, before your eyes and under your nose. Place your trust in him and in his commandments.

You don't have to wait for heaven to draw near to God, to experience his love, and to do his will. Everything you need is available by faith and grace. God has given you the tools to know him—Scripture, prayer, communities of faithful believers, acts of love, peace, and mercy. All of these pull you toward your true center and spiritual home with God. The foretastes of heaven are abundant if you open your heart to see them.

I extol you, my God and
King, and bless your name
forever and ever.

PSALM 145:1 NRSV

God, open my eyes to see
your goodness and mercy in
the midst of this life. Thank
you for giving me a taste of
the good things yet to come.
Amen.

# GOD IS LOVE

*The LORD watches over all who love him.*

PSALM 145:20 NRSV

The New Testament reduces the laws of the Old Testament to one overriding rule: love. If you want to know what true love is, you only need to study God's behavior toward you. God is generous, forbearing, kind, faithful, supportive, nurturing, forgiving, and just. He is everything you want and need.

You exist in God and know God through your own acts of love in the world. He is in the face of everyone you reach out to, no matter from what station in life he or she might come. His love is in your gentle word to a friend in pain, in the simple work of making a home for your family, and in the kindness you show to a stranger. When you live in love, you become more and more like God.

How I love your laws! How
I enjoy your commands!

PSALM 119:47 TLB

God, fill my heart with love for
you and for those whose lives I
touch each day. Thank you for
first loving me and showing
me how to love others.
Amen.

# GOD REVEALS HIMSELF IN YOUR DAILY LIFE

*Those who are wise will take all this to heart:*
*They will see in our history the faithful love of*
*the LORD.*

PSALM 107:43 NLT

Although you sometimes feel that you are alone and he is far away, God is not a distant power. He is an active presence in your life. When you develop the habit of reading the tone and incidents of your days as if he shaped them, you gain insight into how to draw closer to him.

Things don't just happen. Those things you may call "accidents," "surprises," or "discoveries" are actually revelations of God's love and constant concern for you. If you keep your faith and trust in God, the meaning of these things will be become clear. If you greet each new day and expect it to reveal the glory, power, and love of God, your hours will be filled with joy and awe. His mystery will lead you toward him.

I remember the days of old, I
think about all your deeds, I
meditate on the work
of your hands.

PSALM 143:5 NRSV

God, help me see your hand in
all the events of my life. I
know you are with me, giving
my life meaning and purpose.
Amen.

# YOUR HOPE IS IN GOD

*Happy are those who have the God of Israel as their helper, whose hope is in the LORD their God.*

PSALM 146:5 NLT

Hope is a quality you are so accustomed to living with that only in its absence do you truly understand its importance. Hope is what enables you to get out of bed in the morning and get your family off to school and work. Hope is the strength in your backbones that allows you to withstand storms of trouble and pain. Hope keeps you going.

Your grounds for hope is in God's Word and in his promises, in the history of steadfast love he has shown toward you and in the constant care and comfort he gives to all who trust in him. Hope is your reliance on God's blessing and provision for you. Hope puts the smile on your face as you go forward with patience, courage, confidence, and stability.

I will keep on hoping for you to help me; I will praise you more and more. I will tell everyone about your righteousness. All day long I will proclaim your saving power. For I am overwhelmed by how much you have done for me.

PSALM 71:14–15 NLT

God, I want to put you first in my life. Keep your hand on me and don't let me stray from your will, for you are the source of my hope.
Amen.

# PATIENCE AS YOU WAIT ON THE LORD

*I wait for the LORD, my soul waits, and in his word I hope.*

PSALM 130:5–6 NRSV

No one likes to be kept waiting. *The hold button on telephones ought to be outlawed,* you

might sometimes think. The line at a popular restaurant, the crowded waiting room of a doctor's office, the plumber who is late, a lunch date who keeps you waiting—these are all time wasters.

But waiting on God is a different matter. You may go through periods during which you feel he isn't listening to your prayers. Though you ardently beseech him, heaven is silent. During those times, it's important to understand that the "wait" is part of the answer God gives to you. Waiting is part of the mystery of his plan and the degrees by which it will be unfolded to you. God answers you in his time, not yours.

I waited patiently for God to
help me; then he listened
and heard my cry.

PSALM 40:1 TLB

God, help me to be patient
and to rest comfortably in the
knowledge that you are taking
care of all those things that
concern me.
Amen.

# THE GIFT OF GIVING

*He is ever merciful, and lends; And his descendants are blessed.*

PSALM 37:26 NKJV

Giving generously from the heart is extremely satisfying for many reasons, but the most important reason is that it glorifies God. When you give freely, you are acknowledging the abundant, unreserved generosity he has poured out on you, his children. Everything you have, everything, is a gift of God—the clothes on your back, the food on your table, the roof over your head, the color of your eyes, the size of your feet.

There are many ways to give to others and to give back to God. Money is often the first thing that comes to mind; but the gift of time often may be an even greater sacrifice. No matter how you choose to give, you can be sure that God is pleased and will pour out his grace on you in return.

You are the Fountain of life;
our light is from your light.
Pour out your unfailing love
on those who know you!
Never stop giving your
blessings to those who long
to do your will.

PSALM 36:9–10 TLB

God, open my heart and
open my hands to share all
you have given me.
Amen.

# MAKING A SANCTUARY FOR THE SPIRIT

*Our God, here in your temple we think about your love.*

PSALM 48:9 CEV

Some people find that designating a specific time and creating a particular place to meet with God helps them bring more focus and consistency to their quiet time. It is good advice. Some people like to set aside time in the morning. But any time of the day or night will work just fine. Where you meet with God each day is also a matter of personal choice. It can be anywhere, inside or outside, if it is quiet, peaceful, and conducive to reflection and meditation.

Although you pray throughout the day, and even are instructed to pray "constantly," having a little retreat from the world's cares is a great boost for your prayer life. A retreat can bring the full attention of your heart and mind to God.

I wake up early in the morning and cry out. I hope in your word. I stay awake all night so I can think about your promises.

PSALM 119:147–148 NCV

God, thank you for meeting me whenever I come before you. Let me leave the world behind as I bask in the wonder of your love for me. Amen.

# THE LORD RENEWS AND REFRESHES YOUR LIFE

*With You is the fountain of life; In Your light we see light.*

PSALM 36:9 NKJV

As the psalm says, God is the fountain of life, and by his light you see light. He is the source of all good things, and it is your privilege to go to him for nurturing and encouragement, day after day. Your regeneration in God is a lifelong affair.

God is the light by which you see the world and yourself. God is the light through which you understand your reason for being. God is the author of your existence, the creator of your ability to see his light. His light discloses to you the drama of all that he has created. Stay close to his light. If you stray from his light, your world will be plunged into darkness. His light will enable you to fulfill the purpose for which you were created.

I will never forget thy precepts: For with them thou
hast quickened me.

PSALM 119:93 KJV

God, help me stay close to
you, returning day after day
for strength and refreshment
of your love and care.
Amen.

# ALL CREATION PRAISES GOD

*All creation, come praise the name of the LORD.*
*Praise his name alone.*

PSALM 148:13 CEV

In the fullness of summer, in all of its green lushness, you can sometimes hear a noisy symphony of natural sounds. Crickets, frogs, cicadas, birds, dogs, and cows all contribute to the song of praise to God the Creator. How can they keep from singing?

The other seasons have their own harmonies and melodies of praise. In autumn the owl at night and the crow in the morning raise their voices in the crisp breezes; deer, rabbits, raccoons, and other game rustle in the dry foliage. Winter's cool silence and keening winds make their own frosty music, slow and majestic. Then spring, on the rebound from winter's solemnity, sings in full throat with the sounds of a schoolyard at recess. Praise is a natural activity that issues from life filled with God.

Shout to the LORD, all the earth.
Serve the LORD with joy; come
before him with singing.

PSALM 100:1–3 NCV

God, my heart is filled with praise
and my lips with thanksgiving. I
am in awe of your creation.
Thank you for your tender care
over all that you have made.
Amen.

# PRAYER IN A DRY SEASON

*Why am I discouraged? Why so sad? I will put
my hope in God!*

PSALM 43:5 NLT

Occasionally you may experience spiritual dry spells, which can be precipitated by the

loss of a loved one, a personal
defeat, or any number of adverse
circumstances. During those
uncomfortable, barren times, it
often becomes difficult to pray.
God may seem like a vague idea to
you rather than a living reality.

It is comforting to bear in
mind that this is not an unusual occurrence.
Many of the heroes of the faith have experienced the same loss of direction and have had
their faith tested. Even the psalmist David was
afflicted by notorious depressions brought on
by treachery, betrayal, adversaries, and his
own sins. The important thing is not to give
up. You must persist in prayer. Faith and vitality will return. God does not forsake you.

Give ear to my prayer, O God,
And do not hide Yourself from
my supplication. Attend to me,
and hear me; I am restless in my
complaint, and moan noisily.

PSALM 55:1–2 NKJV

God, I know there will be times
when my faith is tested and I
cannot feel you as near as I do
right now. When those times
come, I know that you will
never leave me or forsake me.
Amen.

faith hope

moments of peace in the presence of God

*love*

You have filled my
heart with greater joy
than when their grain
and new wine abound.

PSALM 4:7 NIV

*joy*

# THE DIVINE MYSTERY AT THE HEART OF LIFE

*Such knowledge is too wonderful for me, too great for me to know!*

PSALM 139:6 NLT

God's power and love are too great for you to fully comprehend in this life. Great art, poetry, and music perhaps best convey God's mind-numbing majesty. When you pause from your daily routine of activities, struck by the intensity of a sunset or majesty of a tree or the beauty of a butterfly, you catch a glimpse of the divine mystery at the heart of life. And it only whets your appetite for more. It is a glimmer of God's handiwork, vanishing as quickly as it has captured your attention.

The attitude of awe is a powerful reminder of your littleness and God's greatness. Reacquire the receptive mind of the child so that you may never lose the "wow" you feel for the stunning beauty of God's grandeur in the world.

O give thanks to the Lord of lords, for his steadfast love endures forever; who alone does great wonders, for his steadfast love endures forever.

PSALM 136:3–4 NRSV

God, give me the heart of a child, a heart that is constantly amazed and awed by your greatness. Amen.

# GOD'S LOVE MAKES YOU WEALTHY

*See the one who would not take refuge in God,
but trusted in abundant riches, and sought refuge
in wealth!*

PSALM 52:7 NRSV

You are constantly bombarded with the message that you should want more, buy more, have more. Doing so will bring you happiness, you are told. Potential acquisitions are depicted not only as desirable but essential. You are encouraged to acquire a bigger house and a finer car. You are urged to use your credit cards as you fill those houses to the brim with purchases you often neither really want nor need.

Ultimately "things" can never really satisfy you. As soon as you have acquired a certain possession, the novelty begins to wear off, and you begin to yearn for something else. Start now to live a life in which God is the center. His love is the wealth you truly want, and only in him will you find peace.

They that trust in their wealth, and boast themselves in the multitude of their riches; None of them can by any means redeem his brother, nor give to God a ransom for him.

PSALM 49:6–7 KJV

God, help me to remember that "things" cannot satisfy the deep longing in my heart that can only be filled by you. Amen.

# ACCEPTING THE LORD'S GUIDANCE

*The LORD says, "I will make you wise and show you where to go. I will guide you and watch over you."*

PSALM 32:8 NCV

When you are close to God, regularly praying, studying the Scriptures, and seeking his counsel, you are primed and attuned to the guidance he is offering for your life. As you are paying attention to him, you notice that he is paying attention to you. You begin to experience a calming of your anxieties and an understanding that you don't have to solve your problems alone. You're not in this life alone.

Your thoughts and feelings are honed to pick up his direction and advice in your everyday activities as well as in major decisions and challenges. God's Spirit whispers to you throughout the day, inspiring you to choose wisely and behave properly. Your emotions are at peace, and you are open to receive blessings in your work and family.

You will keep on guiding me
with your counsel, leading
me to a glorious destiny.
Whom have I in heaven but
you? I desire you more than
anything on earth.

PSALM 73:24–25 NLT

God, I look to you for direction
and counsel as I make important
decisions in my life. Give me a
listening ear to hear your voice
and a heart that is quick to obey.
Amen.

# FINDING YOUR LIFE IN GOD

*O taste and see that the LORD is good: blessed is the man that trusteth in him.*

PSALM 34:8 KJV

The central questions in life—Who am I? What am I? Why was I born?—are troubling until you find the answers that ring true for you. These questions can be difficult for those who have no foundation in faith. Being human, you require meaning in your life; and if you do not find it, you are sometimes tempted to feel that life is not worth the effort.

You can only find the answers to these questions as you grow in your relationship with God. God is the one who made you, and he is the one who holds the key to your life. He will reveal to you the purpose for which you were created. You discover that you are God's child and an heir to all his love and grace and mercy.

Let thy mercy, O LORD, be upon us, according as we hope in thee.

PSALM 33:22 KJV

Thank you, God, for creating me and giving my life meaning and purpose. Your love makes all the difference. Amen.

# BELIEVE IN MIRACLES

*The Lord has done this wonderful miracle for me. . . . I shall live! Yes, in his presence—here on earth!*

PSALM 116:7, 9 TLB

Miracles happen every day. Some are extraordinary acts of God that alter the natural course of events, and some consist of situations where individuals have overcome tremendous odds to achieve their goals. But no matter how you define them, miracles happen. No situation is so dire, no goal so remote, that you cannot expect God's help and intervention on your behalf.

Miracles are unexplainable, but so are the other aspects of your relationship with God. You don't know why God loves you unconditionally and completely, but he does. You don't know why he listens to and answers your prayers, but he does. You don't know how miracles happen any more than you know how God created you in the first place. But you don't have to understand; you only have to believe.

I sought the LORD, and he
answered me, and delivered
me from all my fears.

PSALM 34:4 NRSV

God, thank you for the
miracles you have brought to
my life. As I look around me, I
see all that you have done and
I am humbled by your
goodness to me.
Amen.

# SHH, LISTEN

*O rider in the heavens, the ancient heavens;*
*listen, he sends out his voice, his mighty voice.*
PSALM 68:33 NRSV

Of the five senses given to you, listening may be the one most poorly used. Yet it is the key to real communication with others. Often when you ask questions, you may already have formulated the answers you expect. When you engage in conversation, you may often have preconceived ideas of what you are going to hear. Conditioned by habit or limited thinking, your expectations may drown out what is new and interesting.

If you are to respond with your best self to the world, you have to dust off your hearing skills and turn up the volume. You have to pay attention to the pauses between words, the sighs, the tones of voice coming your way. You have to let the sounds of life get through to you.

They speak without a sound or a word; their voice is silent in the skies; yet their message has gone out to all the earth, and their words to all the world.

PSALM 19:3–4 NLT

God, open my ears to hear the sounds around me—the sounds that wake me to the beauty and grandeur of your wonderful world.
Amen.

# AT PEACE WITH THE WORLD IN GOD

*He makes me to lie down in green pastures;*
*He leads me beside the still waters. He*
*restores my soul.*

PSALM 23:2–3 NKJV

Trying to live without God is unimaginably self-defeating. Living without God makes you vulnerable to every sting, swipe, and bludgeon that may come your way. Despite all the intelligence and cunning that God has gifted you with, if you do not rest in God and place all your hope in him, you won't succeed at anything you do. Failure is impossible with God.

Without God in your life, demons of self-doubt can goad you and undermine your best efforts. Anxiety can eat at you and leave you an easy prey for despair and defeat. Fear and trembling accompany you wherever you go. But with God you are safe and secure. You are swathed in a glow of love and peace. You are able to become all he intended you to be.

Only God gives inward
peace, and I depend on him.

PSALM 62:5 CEV

God, thank you for giving me
victory over the world through
my relationship with you. No
longer will I be victimized by
my own weakness, for when I
am weak, you are strong.
Amen.

# THE FORGIVING HEART

*Look on my affliction and my pain, And forgive all my sins.*

PSALM 25:18 NKJV

Someone once said that forgiveness is not for the forgiven, but for the sake of the forgiver. Forgiving those who have wronged you  brings a deeper understanding of the character of God. Forgiveness is the cornerstone of relationship with him. When you hold a grudge, you keep God at a distance. When you let it go, you are restored to him instantly and inner peace returns. He forgets there was ever a rift between you.

If you are struggling today, you can release your right to be angry and release the desire to pass sentence on the one who hurt you, for no one is beyond God's forgiveness. That's the wonder of his mercy. Follow his example and erase the record of wrongs. It takes courage, but it will free you to experience amazing joy.

Create in me a clean heart, O God. Renew a right spirit within me.

PSALM 51:10 NLT

God, help me understand your compassion and mercy. Help me see others as you see them, and turn my thoughts and actions toward forgiveness. Amen.

# GOD'S TENDER MERCIES

*The LORD is good to all: and his tender mercies are over all his works.*

PSALM 145:9 KJV

No one knows you like God; every secret wish, shameful weakness, latent talent, or  buried pain is plainly displayed before him. He loves you in the fullness of who you are, forgiving you of every sin, protecting you from every adversity. He is there to pick you up and dust you off. He is there to guard and protect you.

You may think you need more money; he may know that what you really need is to reorient your priorities. You may be disappointed because you didn't get a job or you missed an opportunity; he may know that what you think you need is not in your best interest. His mercies are mighty. If you let him, he salves all your hurts in an intimate, knowing, and kind way.

Surround me with your tender mercies so I may live, for
your law is my delight.

PSALM 119:77 NLT

God, I place myself in your
care and thank you for your
tender love that brings me all
that you know I need.
Amen.

# A TIME FOR REST

*With all my heart, I will celebrate, and I can safely rest.*

PSALM 16:9 CEV

Rest is a variety of activities that includes loafing, goofing off, hanging out, wandering around, sauntering, and killing time. Rest is  that restorative time where you play, leaving obligations and responsibilities on your desk for a while. You just let things happen. You go for undirected walks in your imaginations where you are like a small child, ready for the next adventure to turn up.

For a while you can let go of your cares and skip along behind God. Who knows what will happen? You can wear a different pair of spectacles that let you see things as if they were new. You can be like a butterfly on a summer morning. Doing nothing can revive a waning spirit, and it's best done in the security and comfort of God's love.

You let me rest in fields of
green grass. You lead me to
streams of peaceful water,
and you refresh my life.

PSALM 23:2–3 CEV

God, teach me to let myself
rest in your love and care,
releasing every burden to you.
Amen.

# JOY

*Heart, body, and soul are filled with joy. . . . You have let me experience the joys of life and the exquisite pleasures of your own eternal presence.*

PSALM 16:9, 11 TLB

Joy is the gift of the Good News. The joy of the Good News beats ice cream, the best movie, mountain climbing, sky diving, the Super Bowl, a hole-in-one, an Oscar. Joyful people whistle, sing, dance, clap, smile, laugh, hoot, holler, turn flips, hop up and down, turn somersaults, and fly through the air in their dreams like Superman.

Joyful people are people on the move; arms and legs, hearts and souls, whirling, they rip through the world repeating everywhere what they've heard. Joy is the jubilant chorus all living things make singing the praises of God. Joy is the thank-you, thank-you, thank-you from the bottom of your heart that erupts when you are put in touch with what really matters. Joy is the irrepressible buoyancy you feel when you have been forgiven.

I will be glad, yes, filled with
joy because of you. I will sing
your praises, O Lord God.

PSALM 9:2 TLB

God, thank you for filling
my heart and life with joy.
Amen.

faith hope

moments of peace in the presence of God

*love*

The LORD is just
in all his ways,
and kind in
all his doings.
PSALM 145:17 NRSV

*kindness*

# HEAVEN

*When I awake in heaven, I will be fully satisfied,*
*for I will see you face to face.*

PSALM 17:15 TLB

You use the word *heaven* to refer to the joyous fulfillment of the purpose of your life—union with God. Certainly life offers you many fleeting foretastes of heaven, yet your present life is truly only preparation for the ultimate reward God has for you. All the pain, care, and imperfections of life will fall away. The restless yearning that goads and prods you will be gone at last. You and your loved ones will be permanently reunited. All your errors will be forgiven. All distance between you and love will be erased.

You will have perfect rest and happiness and complete freedom from want and anxiety. Let heaven keep you going as you allow God's unbreakable promise to lead you through this life to the joy that is in him.

God is good, and he loves
goodness; the godly
shall see his face.

PSALM 11:7 TLB

God, thank you for heaven
and all that it holds for me
and for those I love.
Amen.

# YOUR THANKFULNESS
# AND PRAISE TO GOD

*Clap your hands, all you peoples; shout to God with loud songs of joy. For the LORD, the Most High, is awesome, a great king over all the earth.*
                                    PSALM 47:1–2 NRSV

It's easy to forget to be grateful, to let daily worries distract you from the abundance that

is yours. Mortgage payments, troublesome children, a looming deadline, a broken water heater, a headache, even a burned pizza or a fallen cake can interfere with your appreci-

ation for the blessings you have been given. Inconveniences will pass, but God's blessings and love will keep showering down on you.

Open all your prayers with the praise and thanksgiving that are God's due. When you wake in the morning and before you fall asleep at night, make praise and thanksgiving your first and last thoughts. For whatever your circumstances may be, God has in fact given you the gift of abundant life in the here and now and the promise of life everlasting in the future.

Your great love reaches to the
skies, your truth to the heavens.
God, you are supreme above
the skies. Let your glory
be over all the earth.

PSALM 108:4–5 NCV

Lord, I am rich in love and
comfort, and my heart is
full to the brim. I praise you
and thank you for all you
have given me.
Amen.

# GOD'S DIRECTION AND CORRECTION

*I will instruct thee and teach thee in the way
which thou shalt go: I will guide thee with
mine eye.*

PSALM 32:8 KJV

A true friend cares enough to risk telling you the truth when you've messed up. His or her words may be tough ones, but they will be motivated by love because your friend has your best interest at heart. That's exactly how it is with God. His desire is never to trounce on you, but to bring your heart closer to him.

You may be unaware that you have veered off course. Correction may be a tug on your conscience, a gentle reminder to get back on the right road. God can give you new direction, designed for you. If you're tempted to slip into self-pity over your flubs, draw near to God. Ask, "What do you want me to learn from this?" God is the best friend you'll ever have.

Help me to do your will, for you
are my God. Lead me in good
paths, for your Spirit is good.

PSALM 143:10 TLB

God, help me yield myself to you and
see correction as a way to build my
character, to prepare me for helping
others to trust you more.
Amen.

# GOD LIGHTENS YOUR CARES AND BURDENS

*Commit everything you do to the Lord. Trust him to help you do it, and he will.*

PSALM 37:5 TLB

Keeping a journal can be an enhancement to your spiritual life. You may write in it

every day, or you may simply write often enough to record those things that are uppermost on their mind. The act of writing down your worries and cares is liberating and exhilarating, for it forces you to examine and articulate the sources of your anxiety. When you

identify and analyze these sources of anxiety and ultimately commit them to God, they lose their power over you.

Journaling your worries to God is an effective discipline for reducing stress. In a way, it is like writing God a letter and asking him to take care of things. Once you have done so, you can go about the day relieved and refreshed that you have dealt with your troubles effectively.

Why am I discouraged? Why
am I restless? I trust you!

PSALM 42:5 CEV

God, I release my concerns to
you as I write them down.
Thank you for caring for me
so much that you are con-
cerned with each entry no
matter how great or small.
Amen.

# THE DISCIPLINE OF DAILY PRAYER

*Each morning I will look to you in heaven and lay my requests before you, praying earnestly.*
PSALM 5:3 TLB

Although prayer can be elaborate and formal, prayer requires only simple words about your heart's concerns. Make it a simple matter of regularly setting aside time to talk to God. A daily prayer habit will help you grow spiritually and draw you into a close and comforting relationship with God. These regular activities can be exciting opportunities to interact with the Creator of the universe and influence the world around you.

You can enhance your prayer habit by finding a quiet place with a pleasant atmosphere to regularly meet with God. It's a good idea also to keep a Bible, a journal, and a few inspirational books in that special place. If you are faithful to make yourself available and attentive to God each day, you will reap abundant spiritual dividends.

Let my prayer be like incense placed before you, and my praise like the evening sacrifice.

PSALM 141:2 NCV

God, help me to spend time with you every day talking to you in prayer. Help me make prayer a habit in my life— one that will bless me and draw me closer to you. Amen.

# INVITING GOD INTO YOUR HOME

*My soul shall be satisfied as with marrow and fatness; and my mouth shall praise thee with joyful lips: When I remember thee upon my bed.*

PSALM 63:5–6 KJV

Home is the center of family life and a reflection of who you are and who you hope to become. Home is where you are fully yourself. Home is a haven from the world and its distractions, threats, and annoyances. Just as the home is the center of family life, so God should be the center of your home.

You invite God into your home as you look to him in prayer, personally, and as a family group. You invite him in as you read the Bible and apply its words to your interactions with those nearest and dearest to your heart. You invite him in as you fill your home with symbols of your faith that provide inspiration and comfort. Let God be the head of your home rather than a convenient guest.

Your kindness and love will always be with me each day of my life, and I will live forever in your house, LORD.

PSALM 23:6 CEV

God, come into my home. Dwell with me through the good times and the bad. Show me how to live my life to the fullest through your indwelling presence. Amen.

# GOD DISPELS CONFUSION AND DOUBT

*Pray to me in time of trouble. I will rescue you, and you will honor me.*

PSALM 50:15 CEV

You have probably experienced the disruption and confusion of moving to a new home, with all your worldly goods packed and transported from the order and familiarity of your old home to the unfamiliar chaos of your new one. It can be disorienting and stressful to have to search for the items necessary to the conduct of your life. If only you had a map showing where everything was packed away.

God has provided a map for your life. His commandments and teachings give you the meaning and clarity you need to live peacefully and productively. If you are momentarily confused or doubtful, you can call on him and he will help you find what you need to carry on. God is right there, waiting for an invitation to step in and set things right.

O send out thy light and thy truth: let them lead me; Let them bring me unto thy holy hill, and to thy tabernacles.

PSALM 43:3 KJV

God, when I experience times of confusion and doubt, help me remember that you are there waiting to comfort and guide me.
Amen.

# GRACE SUFFICIENT FOR THE HOUR

*The LORD is gracious and full of compassion, Slow to anger and great in mercy. The LORD is good to all, And His tender mercies are over all His works.*

PSALM 145:8–9 NKJV

Grace is God's favor, unmerited. Grace is God's mercy, undeserved. Grace is God's compassion, boundless. This wondrous gift of grace comes to you because you are fortunate enough to be God's child. And because you are his, he loves you unconditionally.

Grace is your birthright as a child of God. You fully avail yourself to this bounty by placing your complete trust in him. You have access to his grace by having confidence in his promises. When you act on this confidence in God, you find that nothing is too great a challenge, no obstacle too large to overcome. Though you may approach a tough situation with trepidation, knowing the limitations of your own meager abilities, you can ask for God's help and be certain that he will give it.

You are merciful, LORD! You
are kind and patient and
always loving. You are good
to everyone, and you take
care of all your creation.

PSALM 145:8–9 CEV

God, help me open my eyes to
the heritage you have given
me as your child. Thank you
especially for protecting and
supporting me at all times.
Amen.

# CLAIMING GOD'S BLESSINGS

*He fills my life with good things.*

PSALM 103:5 NLT

God's blessings are available to you as you put your trust in him and keep his command-

ments. His abundance is beautiful and simple. His promises are everywhere in Scripture. He will be your God if you will be his child; if you honor and obey him, he will withhold nothing from you. All you have to do is ask.

God forgives your trespasses and provides righteousness and justice when you are treated unfairly; he is merciful and gracious; he is slow to get angry and full of unfailing love. Sin and despair are the only obstacles between you and God's many blessings. They can cloud your vision and prevent you from seeing things as they are. But God understands and is eternally patient with you. He will give you the grace to overcome your weaknesses.

See for yourself the way his
mercies shower down on all
who trust in him. If you
belong to the LORD,
reverence him; for everyone
who does this has
everything he needs.

PSALM 34:8–9 TLB

God, thank you for the
blessings you have placed in
my life. Cleanse my heart so
that I can receive all you
have provided for me.
Amen.

# PEOPLE ARE TO BE HELPED, NOT SHUNNED

*Good and upright is the LORD; Therefore He teaches sinners in the way.*

PSALM 25:8 NKJV

When you were a child, your parents warned you to stay away from "bad" companions who might cause you to stray from the right path. Certainly this was and is good advice for the very young and the easily influenced.

But you learn from Scripture that God loves all his children and wants you to be united with him. You also learn that as a believer you have a responsibility to be a blessing not only to those who are living godly lives but also to those who are not. You are a mirror of God's love in the world; you reflect and pass along the goodness and mercy shown to you. And you practice this commandment most notably when you reach out to people who do not know that God loves them.

Who can understand his errors? Cleanse me from secret faults. Keep back Your servant also from presumptuous sins; Let them not have dominion over me.

PSALM 19:12–13 NKJV

God, give me the courage to reach out to those who do not yet know you. Give me the words to speak truth and love into their lives.

Amen.

# THE HEALING POWER OF GOD

*O LORD my God, I cried to you for help, and you have healed me.*

PSALM 30:2 NRSV

Prayer is good medicine. It's a fact, and medical science has finally caught on. Studies show that when you pray regularly and com-

mit your welfare to God, you recover from serious illness and trauma faster than those who have no faith in God. Your outlook on life is more positive; your hope for the future is stronger. And as far as minor illnesses are

concerned, you even get fewer colds than those who face life without the advantage of genuine faith.

Prayer and thanksgiving relieve stress, alleviate anxiety, promote positive thinking, and generally foster happiness and contentment. Is it any wonder that such things contribute to your health? When you know that God is in charge of everything and is your guide, you are less likely to take yourself too seriously.

Come, O Lord, and make me
well. In your kindness save me.

PSALM 6:4 TLB

God, faith is so important to
every aspect of my life.
Without it, I would be lonely
and without hope. Thank you
for being there to hear me
when I pray.
Amen.

# WHEN CLOUDS COME

*I am old now; I have lived a long time, but I have never seen good people abandoned by the LORD or their children begging for food.*

PSALM 37:25 GNT

A mother and her son stood before a statue of Christ on a mountaintop that loomed over a large city. The statue had outstretched arms reaching downward in an act of blessing. It was so beautiful to the little boy as the sun shone brightly around it and the blue sky set a peacefully serene backdrop. Suddenly clouds moved in, and no one could see the statue. This upset the little boy. He clutched his mother's hand and gasped a loud sigh. "Mommy, what happened to him? Where did he go?" His mother smiled and spoke warmly to her son, "Oh, honey, he's still there. He never goes away."

God's presence is not predicated on your awareness of it. No amount of inattention on your part erases the company God keeps with you.

I have relied on you all my life; you have protected me since the day I was born. I will always praise you.

PSALM 71:6 GNT

Dear God, thank you for paying attention to me even when I don't pay attention to you. Your faithfulness gives me a great and wonderful peace.
Amen.

# TAKING THE ROLL

*The LORD gives strength to his people; The LORD blesses his people with peace.*

PSALM 29:11 NIV

A small group of peasants met for worship in a country where religious gatherings were banned. In the midst of their service, a door burst open and a contingent of grim soldiers marched into the room. The leader of the soldiers shouted to one of his subordinates to take the names of everyone in the room. After the names were written down, an old peasant spoke up, "Sir, there's one name you didn't get." The officer barked that the old man was wrong, but he insisted and the officer reluctantly conceded, "All right then, who is it we don't have on the list?" The old man responded confidently, "The Lord Jesus Christ, he is here."

Jesus Christ is risen to be with you in all places. Nothing anyone can say or do to you changes that.

Lead me, O LORD, in your righteousness because of my enemies; make your way straight before me.

PSALM 5:8 NRSV

Dear God, your presence brings peace to me when some people bring discontent. I know you are present to love and protect me no matter what happens. Amen.

# A NEW NAME

*He put a new song in my mouth, a song of praise to our God; Many will see and fear And will trust in the LORD.*

PSALM 40:3 NASB

There is a town in England named Christchurch, and it received its name in a most interesting way. Many years ago, some men were building a church there and were joined in their work by a stranger who was an excellent carpenter. He worked

harder than anyone else but would never accept any pay. When the church was completed, a dedication service was held, but the stranger did not attend. He was never seen in their town again. As the townspeople pondered this mystery, they decided the stranger was none other than Jesus, the carpenter from Nazareth. After only a little deliberation, they voted to change the name of their town from Twineham to Christchurch.

When Jesus comes to your heart, nothing stays the same. He revives you and then he revises you.

Create in me a clean heart, O God, and put a new and right spirit within me.

PSALM 51:10 NRSV

Dear God, you change my fear to faith, my reluctance to resolve, and my uneasiness to peace. I give thanks for your transforming power in my life. Amen.

# OUT OF HARM'S WAY

*He made my feet like the feet of a deer, and set me secure on the heights.*

PSALM 18:33 NRSV

One day a fire broke out in Thomas Edison's laboratory and burned it to the  ground, destroying many valuable and unfinished experiments. Later that day, walking through the charred wreckage, Edison collected various items and put them in a bag he carried. Among those items was a little package of papers tied tightly together with a thick string. The package, although fire scarred and water soaked, was intact. Edison opened it and at its center was a photograph of himself. It was scorched around the edges but basically undamaged. He looked at it for a minute, then pulled a piece of charred wood from the floor and wrote across the picture: "It didn't touch me."

No matter what happens to you, God can ease the pounding of your heart by the quieting of your mind.

Then they were glad because
they had quiet, and he
brought them to their
desired haven.

PSALM 107:30 NRSV

Dear God, you slow me
down and send my roots
deep into the soil of your love
and grace. Thank you.
Amen.

# GOD'S ERASER

*O LORD, rescue my soul;*
*Save me because of Your lovingkindness*
PSALM 6:4 NASB

A Sunday school teacher was using a chalkboard to illustrate the story of Jesus walking on the water and calming the sea. She  drew huge storm clouds spitting out lots of wind and rain. She told the children how frightened the disciples of Jesus were. Then she drew huge waves wildly rocking their little boat. Next she created on the chalkboard a shoreline and put Jesus walking from there toward the disciples on the water. Then she replaced the storm clouds and all their havoc with a bright moon and glowing stars. "Why do you think the storm went away and the water got calm?" she asked the children. One precocious child responded, "Because you erased them!"

God's presence in your life erases the storms brought to you by others and by yourself. When you feel God's presence, you are assured of all the help he brings.

Be gracious to me, O God, be gracious to me, For my soul takes refuge in You; And in the shadow of Your wings I will take refuge, Until destruction passes by.

PSALM 57:1 NASB

Dear God, thank you for the peace at the center of my life when I acknowledge your presence. When you are here, peace is near.
Amen.

# EVERYWHERE YOU ARE

*You have enclosed me behind and before,*
*And laid Your hand upon me.*

PSALM 139:5 NASB

Having returned from Sunday school, a little boy was playing with his dog in the front yard of his house. A neighbor, the  local cynic, walked by and stopped to visit with the boy. He asked him what he'd been doing that morning, and the boy told him he'd been to Sunday school, where he'd learned a lot about God. The neighbor laughed derisively and challenged the boy, "Well, if you can tell me where God is, I'll give you a quarter." The boy responded in a polite and calm voice, "Sir, if you'll tell me where God isn't, I'll give you a dollar."

God is everywhere you are. For the most difficult day, God is your stay. For the darkest night, God is your light. God is with you in all things to bring you peace.

Let me hear what God the
LORD will speak, for he will
speak peace to his people.

PSALM 85:8 NRSV

Dear God, I can't go anywhere
today that you won't be there
to greet me with peace. Thank
you for the peace you give
when I come to you.
Amen.

# faith hope

moments of peace in the presence of God

*love*

I trust in your
unfailing love; my
heart rejoices in
your salvation.
PSALM 13:5 NIV

*love*

# A STEADFAST HEART

*My heart is steadfast, O God; I will sing and make music with all my soul. Awake, harp and lyre! I will awaken the dawn.*

PSALM 108:1–2 NIV

Early morning is a lovely time of day, a time before daily responsibilities demand your attention. Standing on a porch with eyes lifted to the trees, you can easily see why the psalmist chose to "awaken the dawn." Breezes are blowing, colors are varied and vibrant, and life is stirring all around you. Song is filling the air—birds are singing, cicadas are shrilling, crickets are chirping. Do these creatures know instinctively that God put music in their bodies? Do they make melody to him?

Whether you choose to sing aloud your own song to God or to praise him in silence from your heart, God can hear and enjoy the music of a happy soul that is unwavering and resolute in him. Sing and make joyous music to your God.

The birds nest beside the streams and sing among the branches of the trees. You send rain on the mountains from your heavenly home, and you fill the earth with the fruit of your labor.

PSALM 104:12–13 NLT

Dear God, thank you for the song you put in my heart. I will sing it in praise for who you are to me.
Amen.

# THE BEAUTY OF CHANGE

*You set the limits of the earth; you made summer and winter.*

PSALM 74:17 GNT

Almost everyone loves summer, but sometimes you can't see winter's graces at first glance. Ice or slush may mask the grace of skeletal trees that dot the landscape and thin grass that clings to the hard-packed earth. Yes, even in the stark lines of winter, you can see the work of a skillful artist—God, who designed beauty to be dynamic, to renew itself in change.

The seasons are perhaps nature's best example of this. You watch as summer's bright greens give way to fall's warmer palette, then fade into winter's gray and white. Just when you long for the sight of green again, spring comes, bringing once more the buds of change and new life. God must have known you would need visuals to remind you of his purpose in change.

Take a good look at God's
wonders—they'll take your
breath away.

PSALM 66:5 THE MESSAGE

Dear God, thank you for the
changes in my life. May I
receive them as your way of
growing me into what you
want me to be.
Amen.

# STOKING THE FIRE

*Take delight in the LORD, and he will give you your heart's desires.*

PSALM 37:4 NLT

The act of building a fire is filled with anticipation. You choose something easily flammable as a starter and then position each piece of wood in an orderly pattern. You experience a thrill when oxygen feeds the fire and the fuel catches, and you lean back in satisfaction.

Sitting by a fire on a cold night is one of life's simple pleasures. You poke at the embers and watch, fascinated, as the sparks fly upward into the flue and disappear from sight. Just as you can stoke embers into a flame, God gives you constant reminders of himself—a momentary thought, the kindness of a stranger, a smile on a child's face—that stir your heart-fire into a warm, healthy glow. Then, like the sparks that are drawn upward, your thoughts rush to him.

Come and hear, all ye that
fear God, and I will
declare what he hath done
for my soul.

PSALM 66:16 KJV

Dear God, thank you for
all the channels of grace
on which you show
yourself to me. May I
tune in each day.
Amen.

# A CHILDLIKE CONTENTMENT

*I have calmed and quieted my soul, like a weaned child with its mother; my soul is like the weaned child that is with me.*

PSALM 131:2 NRSV

Small children have the ability to go with the moment, their imaginations seizing the opportunities of whatever little joys they happen upon. Nothing is too small or too insignificant for their wonder: a dandelion, a pile of crisp leaves, a tiny worm, or an unexplored mud puddle.

Watching children romp, you're reminded that play is their "work." Play is a time for unleashing imagination and creative energy. The heart of a child seems to embody all that God finds best about humankind. Maybe that's why David likened himself to a "weaned child," gladly deferring thoughts of things "too marvelous" for him to God. What greater image of contentment is there than that of a young child resting with complete trust on the shoulder of the one who loves him best?

You had my mother give birth to me. You made me trust you while I was just a baby. I have leaned on you since the day I was born; you have been my God since my mother gave me birth.

PSALM 22:9–10 NCV

Dear God, I am in awe of your presence everywhere. I will dance before your goodness and sing a song of gladness for your grace. Amen.

# THE GIFT OF FORGIVENESS

*How blessed is he whose transgression is forgiven,*
*Whose sin is covered!*

PSALM 32:1 NASB

The telephone rings, breaking the silence and bringing with it an unexpected gift: the forgiveness of a friend. A friendship is restored. Within seconds, joy replaces the misery that weighed your heart down like overloaded baggage. Your friend's voice and message are balm to your spirit.

Nothing breathes new life into your soul like forgiveness, whether you receive it or give it to another. Amazingly, three small words take on a transforming power the moment they are uttered: *I forgive you.* How blessed you are when you hear these words. Forgiveness wraps you in a contentment that reaches deep into your heart. The most surprising gift of forgiveness is that it triggers a reciprocal response. In the moment you receive forgiveness, you are stirred to "do unto others" the very same thing.

You are kind, God! Please have pity on me. You are always merciful! Please wipe away my sins. Wash me clean from all of my sin and guilt.

PSALM 51:1–2 CEV

Dear God, your forgiveness gets out the stains left behind by me and by others. It is your great delete key in my life. Thank you for so much mercy. Amen.

# A DECISION TO TRUST

*Blessed is the man who makes the LORD his trust,*
*who does not look to the proud, to those who turn*
*aside to false gods.*

PSALM 40:4 NIV

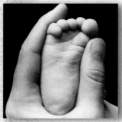

Learning to swim is daunting. You'll probably never forget how it felt to
squint across the pool before filling your lungs with that last
deep breath. Three strokes later,
your hesitant paddling ended in
frantic sputtering when water
started closing over your head.
At the same moment, strong arms caught you
from beneath and lifted you back up to the surface. Dad or Mom had been there all along.

A heart of trust is one of life's sweet but
hard-won gifts. The discovery that God is
always there, ready to lift you up when you start
to sink, replaces fear with courage and timidity
with boldness. Along with that courage and
boldness comes the strength to face whatever life
throws at you—even when it requires a long,
scary swim to the other side.

In You, O Lord, I put my trust; Let me never be ashamed; Deliver me in Your righteousness.

Psalm 31:1 nkjv

Dear God, I am a child in your arms. Thank you for holding me in your loving embrace. I depend on your provision and protection. Amen.

# NO FEAR!

*Yea, though I walk through the valley of the shadow of death, I will fear no evil: for thou art with me; thy rod and thy staff they comfort me.*

PSALM 23:4 KJV

When the line of clothing called No Fear seized the youth market in the mid-1990s, bumper stickers sporting the logo appeared on cars all across the nation. For the uninitiated, the words seemed puzzling. No fear? Why not? But the marketers knew that the designer's slogan would appeal to its street-savvy customers who understood that the slogan represented a gutsy, no-holds-barred approach to a life lived to the extreme.

But God had the meaning of the slogan first. He preempted the popular slogan by several thousand years. He's always been in the no-fear business, giving you comfort in the midst of your darkest hours and guiding you back to the right path when you lose your footing. Bravado can't measure up to the heart that has learned the true meaning of having no fear.

Blessed be the Lord—day after day he carries us along. He's our Savior, our God, oh yes! He's God-for-us, he's God-who-saves-us. LORD GOD knows all death's ins and outs.

PSALM 68:19–20 THE MESSAGE

Dear God, some of my fears are between my ears, but others are real. Help me know the difference. Teach me to respond to real fear in true faith.
Amen.

# THE CONFIDENCE OF ANSWERED PRAYER

*In the day when I cried thou answeredst me, and*
*strengthenedst me with strength in my soul.*

PSALM 138:3 KJV

In the not-too-distant past, parents often summoned children for supper by means of a dinner bell. No matter where the children played, the sound of Mama's bell brought them scrambling toward home. Through the years, the pattern remained the same: Mama called, and the children responded by showing up at the table. It was a summons not just to eat but to come home.

Now you are the one who often does the calling, and you wonder: Does God hear you? Will he answer your prayers? You can have confidence in the fact that God not only hears but is faithful to answer your cries for help. Knowing that God is always ready to respond when you call to him gives you boldness and strength. In him you find your true home.

Hear a just cause, O LORD;
attend to my cry; give ear
to my prayer from lips
free of deceit.

PSALM 17:1 NRSV

God, I am glad I am a
member of your family. I am
listened to and I am heard.
You honor me with your
patience and encourage me
with your faithfulness.
Amen.

# AN ETERNAL PERSPECTIVE

*You will keep on guiding me all my life with your wisdom and counsel, and afterwards receive me into the glories of heaven!*

PSALM 73:24 TLB

High up in the Rockies, downhill skiing is treacherous if a skier diverts from the trail onto unmarked terrain. For this reason, occasional signs are posted to warn extreme skiers not to venture beyond the marked zones. Skiers who ignore the signs risk their lives unnecessarily just to experience a thrill-ride that may cross pits or rocks hidden by blankets of snow.

Signposts, warning lights, directional guides—all were created for one purpose: to keep you safe and out of harm's way. God, too, designed a system to ensure your safety. He promises to guide you through the labyrinth of life, offering his wisdom and divine counsel. Like the skiers, you have the choice to follow those guidelines or to ignore them at your own risk. You are prudent to heed God's wisdom.

Give me understanding,
that I may observe Your law
And keep it with all my
heart. Make me walk in the
path of Your command-
ments, For I delight in it.

PSALM 119:34–35 NASB

Thank you, God, for your
wings under which I am
protected from what
threatens me and by which
I am taken to where you
want me to be.
Amen.

# GOD SATISFIES THE SOUL

*He satisfies the longing soul, And fills the hungry soul with goodness.*

PSALM 107:9 NKJV

Holidays and special occasions are universally celebrated by feasting. Imagine a birthday party without a cake, the Fourth of July without  watermelon, Thanksgiving without pumpkin pie. Sharing food around a table bonds people together, and "Pass the peas, please" branches into warm and meaningful conversation. The sharing of food leads to the sharing of words and the sharing of hearts.

In the same way, when you feast on the goodness of God, which you can do as often as you like, it satisfies your soul-hunger like nothing else can. Out of that fullness comes a desire to feed others with the blessings God has showered on you. When you give out of your abundance, you are filled even more. Your plate is never empty; your soul is always full.

I have trusted in thy mercy; my heart shall rejoice in thy salvation. I will sing unto the LORD, because he hath dealt bountifully with me.

PSALM 13:5–6 KJV

At every meal, God, I am reminded of the many ways you feed my heart. Thank you for the other kind of bread, the kind with which you nourish my very being. Amen.

# FINDING FAVOR WITH GOD

*Keep me as the apple of the eye, hide me under the shadow of thy wings.*

PSALM 17:8 KJV

Parents try never to have favorites among their children. With the birth of each child comes a love tailor-made just for him or her. The biblical David, however, unabashedly assumed he was the apple of God's eye. He assumed he was a favored son. From that place of special favor, he asked for God's protection. In intimate language, he depicted a mother hen covering her hatchlings—whenever startled, the chicks run toward their mother, and she lifts a protective wing to hide them.

You, too, can be a favored child. He lifts a spreading wing to cover you with warmth and safety, and you can take refuge in his protection. Being a favored son or daughter entitles you to the bounty of God's goodness and grace.

Please, LORD, save us;
please, LORD, give us
success. God bless the one
who comes in the name of
the LORD. We bless all of
you from the Temple
of the LORD.

PSALM 118:25–26 NCV

Dear God, you affirm
me in many ways. Your
power upholds me and
your love enfolds me.
You say yes to me even
when I say no to myself.
Amen.

# STRENGTH AND COURAGE

*Be strong, and let your heart take courage, all you who wait for the Lord.*

PSALM 31:24 NRSV

What does it mean to "wait for the Lord"? If you're like most people, you don't like waiting

and wish you never had to. Waiting means deferring your wants and needs—sometimes to the point of inconvenience, but sometimes to the point of despair. Another version translates this verse "all you who hope in the Lord." Hope is

expectation, and it hints at more to come. It's easier to hope than to wait.

Human nature craves quick replies and speedy results, but God's timetable isn't human. God's timetable is different, and it seems to tick more slowly than your own. Perhaps that is why all who hope in the Lord are encouraged to be strong and courageous. Those who wait for God are rewarded with a satisfied heart—a heart of courage.

All day long I will proclaim
your saving power, for I am
overwhelmed by how much
you have done for me.

PSALM 71:15 NLT

Teach me, dear God, the
wisdom of your timing.
Let me know it is in waiting that I am renewed.
Amen.

# THE SHEPHERD'S LEADING

*The LORD is my shepherd; I shall not want. He maketh me to lie down in green pastures: he leadeth me beside the still waters.*

PSALM 23:1–2 KJV

Sheep respond to a voice—especially the voice of their shepherd. Amazingly, some shepherds claim to know the sound of an individual sheep's bleat, even when the sheep calls out from the midst of a large herd. One shepherd named each of her sheep and recognized their voices when they called to her. She attests to the fact that sheep are known also for their instinct to follow. They will follow her wherever she leads, whether high up on a rocky slope, down into a grassy pasture, or back to the paddock for shearing time.

The twenty-third psalm depicts a Good Shepherd who leads you to safety and nourishes the soul. You know that you are safe with the Good Shepherd and that he is keeping watch on the horizon.

Protect me, God, because I trust in you. I said to the LORD, "You are my Lord. Every good thing I have comes from you."

PSALM 16:1–2 NCV

When I follow you, God, I discover both possibility and power. Forgive me for sitting still in my will when I could be moving out in yours. Amen.

# REST FOR THE WEARY

*Oh that I had wings like a dove! for then would I fly away, and be at rest.*

PSALM 55:6 KJV

You have probably experienced the sensation of flying in a dream, floating high above the crowd, and reveled in it. To be like the birds, you think, and just fly away when the world presses in too closely; to experience the heady joy of unrestricted movement. You long to have "wings like a dove," but most of the time you feel more like a chicken, flapping miserably around in the barnyard, unable to get off the ground for sustained flight.

When you are bone-weary and eager to fly away, God can give you rest and sustain you. In that place of physical, emotional, and spiritual exhaustion, a divine paradox emerges: When you are weak, he becomes strong in you. Your very weakness is a tool that magnifies his glory.

He renews my strength.
He guides me along right
paths, bringing honor to
his name.

PSALM 23:3 NLT

Show me, dear God, that
while there is no music in
a rest, there is the making
of music in it. When I rest
in you, I am close to your
power, which becomes my
strength for life.
Amen.

faith hope

moments of peace in the presence of God

*love*

*goodness*

Surely goodness and
mercy shall follow
me all the days of
my life, and I shall
dwell in the house
of the LORD my
whole life long.
PSALM 23:6 NRSV

# INSPIRATION ON HIGH

*Bless the Lord, O my soul; And all that is within me, bless His holy name!*

PSALM 103:1 NKJV

Certain overlooks along the Blue Ridge Parkway demand attention the way a harvest moon draws eyes to the night sky. The scenic route twists and winds for more than four hundred miles along the crests of the Blue Ridge and Smoky Mountain ranges, offering views of stunning peaks and spectacular valleys wrapped in the hazy blue mist that earned the mountains their name. You stop, and your breath catches suddenly in your throat. Your perspective changes as you look out, and your worry diminishes. God's awesome creation lifts your heart.

The dramatic and breathtaking mountain-top panorama inspires you to praise God with your whole being. Your eyes may even mist over in joy. Paradoxically, when you praise him, you are blessed in return. Your spirit is exultant and your heart soars.

Hallelujah! It's a good thing to sing praise to our God; praise is beautiful, praise is fitting.

PSALM 147:1 THE MESSAGE

Dear God, I can only praise you rightly when I praise you for everything. Everywhere I look I see the fingerprints of your glorious touch.
Amen.

# THIRSTING FOR GOD

*A white-tailed deer drinks from the creek; I want
to drink God, deep draughts of God.*

PSALM 42:1 THE MESSAGE

Soft drinks, sweetened iced tea, and flavored
sparkling water rank high on
today's list of preferred bever-
ages. When you're parched
from heat or exercise, however,
the only thing you want is pure
water. The psalmist used the
metaphor of a deer panting for
water to describe his thirst for God. A deer slak-
ing its thirst will sink its muzzle into a stream
long enough to satisfy its craving.

When you thirst deep in your soul, you, like
the deer, instinctively turn to the source that
refreshes—God. You immerse yourself in
prayer; and you search the Scriptures. You listen
for the voice of God and thank God when you
hear it. God fills your need and sustains you for
the task at hand. You drink—and are fortified by
him.

He changes a wilderness into
a pool of water, And a dry
land into springs of water.

PSALM 107:35 NASB

I am thirsty, dear God, for
the living water of your
power and I am hungry
for the eternal bread of
your presence. I gladly
drink and eat at your table.
Amen.

# THE BLESSEDNESS OF HELPING

*Blessed is he that considereth the poor:*
*the LORD will deliver him in time of trouble.*

PSALM 41:1 KJV

Stepping out of the convenience store, you spot him—again. The same man who perched against the window ledge a week ago, flashing a little card asking for money. Over at the discount store, a Salvation Army worker clangs her hand bell rhythmically, scanning the holiday shoppers as they rush past and hoping to meet a pair of friendly eyes.

Giving brings out the best in you and makes you a little bit more like God, the greatest giver of all. Everything you have belongs to God anyway, and you need to decide how much you need to keep and how much you need to give away. When you go through your life with an attitude of giving, you are prompted to help when you're least aware of your helpfulness.

They give generously to
those in need. Their good
deeds will never be
forgotten. They will have
influence and honor.

PSALM 112:9 NLT

Dear God, I will give to
others as you give to
me. I will bless as I am
blessed, knowing that
whatever I give now I
will have forever.
Amen.

# THE REFINER'S FIRE

*God's words are pure words, Pure silver words
refined seven times In the fires of his word-kiln.*
PSALM 12:6 THE MESSAGE

Once a ceramist creates a figure, the object must be baked under extreme heat before it's ready for use. The firing process delays the enjoyment of the object, and yet if the ceramist skips this process, the object will be useless. The beauty and service of the piece are strengthened for having "passed through the fire."

God must refine you, too, through the fires of adversity. Sometimes that refining process takes the shape of waiting; other times that process allows you to suffer losses, great or small. The process may be as mundane as finding contentment in your ordinary life, or it may be as intense as facing a life-threatening illness. In the end, you are rendered more beautiful and useful to God by having passed through the fire.

Happy are those who live pure lives, who follow the LORD's teachings. Happy are those who keep his rules, who try to obey him with their whole heart.

PSALM 119:1–2 NCV

Dear God, when I might say "Why me, Lord?" may I instead say "Try me, Lord." Try me and find in me a hope that hangs on and a faith that clings to. Amen.

# HOPE'S REWARD

*O Lord, you alone are my hope. I've trusted you,*
*O LORD, from childhood.*

PSALM 71:5 NLT

On the heels of World War II, Peter Marshall, the celebrated United States Senate chaplain during the 1940s, offered a famous prayer called "Bifocals of Faith." Before the statesmen of his day, he prayed, "God, give us the faith to believe in the ultimate triumph of righteousness, no matter how dark and uncertain are the skies of today. We pray for the bifocals of faith—that see the despair and the need of the hour but also see, further on, the patience of our God working out his plan in the world he has made."

Hope springs from a heart that trusts in God. Without hope, your life would quickly turn bleak. But with this virtue in your heart, every dark and uncertain sky holds clouds with silver linings.

I find rest in God; only he gives me hope. He is my rock and my salvation. He is my defender; I will not be defeated.

PSALM 62:5–6 NCV

Dear God, I see more with my heart than with my eyes. Through faith, I see your love, encouragement, and purpose. Thank you for what I see. Amen.

# DELIGHT IN HIS WILL

*I delight to do Your will, O my God, And Your law is within my heart.*

PSALM 40:8 NKJV

You mark the arrival of a new year through the simple task of hanging a fresh calendar on the wall. Flipping through the calendar, you may pause to scan the pages of the months ahead and wonder what they hold in store for you. Will March bring a surprise blessing? Will you have an unexpected opportunity in July? Will there be a disappointment in September? What will happen between now and when December rolls around again?

Though you anticipate the future, and sometimes worry about it, God is the one who sets your course and imprints each day with the events that become your life. A heart committed to God can leave the passing of time in his hands and trust that he will fill in the blanks of the calendar with perfect order.

Be delighted with the Lord.
Then he will give you all
your heart's desires.
Commit everything you do
to the Lord. Trust him to
help you do it, and he will.

PSALM 37:4–5 TLB

Dear God, no matter the
circumstances, when I
am in your will I am in a
large place. I fix my
mind and heart now on
doing your will.
Amen.

# REAPING THE JOY

*Sing for joy to God, our strength; shout out loud to the God of Jacob.*

PSALM 81:1 NCV

A trip to the beach on a hot summer day is a ticket to leisure for most folks. Strolling along the shore, you can watch surfers bobbing like corks as they wait for the next big breaker. Giant waves that would scare most swimmers produce a thrill for good surfers, who glide along the waves rather than get pounded by them. In the same way, author Jim Reimann observed that "the things you try to avoid and fight against . . . are the very things that produce abundant joy in you."

True joy, it has been said, is not built on passing things; rather, true joy is built on the unchangeable love of God. Whether the events you face are ordinary or terrifying, they are powerless to separate you from God's love.

Remember me, O Lord, when
you show favor to your people,
come to my aid when you save
them, that I may enjoy the
prosperity of your chosen ones,
that I may share in the joy of
your nation and join your
inheritance in giving praise.

Psalm 106:4–5 niv

Dear God, I believe joy
is the most infallible
sign of your presence in
my life. It is the banner
I fly when you live
in my heart.
Amen.

# FORTIFIED IN SPIRIT

*I will meditate in thy precepts, and have respect unto thy ways. I will delight myself in thy statutes: I will not forget thy word.*

PSALM 119:15–16 KJV

The word *library* calls to mind a variety of images—a large room with floor-to-ceiling shelves, tables with people sitting hunched over their books, numbered signs directing you to a plethora of subjects, a row of computers, a small section devoted to new arrivals, and nothing but the sound of rustling pages, soft hums, and gentle whispers—the sounds of studying. A quiet time of contemplation and study is consoling and satisfying. You feel that you've found some answers you've been seeking.

When the words you meditate on come from God, you are fortified in your spirit as well as your mind. A heart soaked in the knowledge of God changes from the inside out. If you continue to meditate, you will discover that what started as a discipline has turned to a delight.

You made me willing to listen and obey. And so, I said, "I am here to do what is written about me in the book, where it says, I enjoy pleasing you. Your Law is in my heart.'"

PSALM 40:6–8 CEV

Thank you, God, for all the times I hear you speak when I meditate on your word. Through faith and practice, keep me within hearing distance. Amen.

# THE DIVINE GATEKEEPER

*The LORD is thy keeper: the LORD is thy shade upon thy right hand.*

PSALM 121:5 KJV

Throughout history, gatekeepers have filled a crucial role. From their lookout, they could see who was approaching the city and determine whether that person—or group of people—should be allowed inside the city walls. They kept out and ushered in as they saw fit, all with the best interests of the city's inhabitants in mind.

Your step becomes sure when you know that God is your gatekeeper—the one who allows you to come and go in safety. He allows you to pass through. It's comforting to know that this same gatekeeper also bars your entry to any place that might bring you harm. He knows when to open doors and when to close them. With God as your gatekeeper, you need never fear where your foot may fall.

The LORD shall preserve thy
going out and thy
coming in from this time
forth, and even for evermore.

PSALM 121:8 KJV

I praise you, God, that
you are my on-time God.
You come exactly when I
need you, even when I
don't know I need you.
Amen.

# HEALING THE BROKEN HEART

*The LORD is close to the brokenhearted and saves those who are crushed in spirit.*

PSALM 34:18 NIV

A rare, blooming bush takes a long time to cultivate. Even when its buds finally open up and hold their blossoms to the sun, the blooms  can be crushed in an instant. Yet over time, the heart of the bush can be restored, and it can once again sprout new blossoms, sometimes even more beautiful than the first. With tender care, the stalks can grow strong again, capable of sending roots deep into the earth where the bush can find lasting nourishment.

When and how God chooses to comfort you may come as a surprise, but comfort almost always arrives in the form of another human being. The right words, spoken at the right time, lift your broken heart—your broken spirit—and give you hope that life will go on.

May those who sow in tears
reap with shouts of joy.
Those who go out weeping,
bearing the seed for sowing,
shall come home with shouts
of joy, carrying their sheaves.

PSALM 126:5–6 NRSV

Finding and following
your purpose, dear God,
fills me when I am empty,
directs me when I am lost,
and mends me when I am
broken. Thank you.
Amen.

# WAITING FOR GOD'S TIMING

*Truly my soul silently waits for God; From Him comes my salvation.*

PSALM 62:1 NKJV

No amount of worrying can make things happen, let alone make them happen the way

you want. Still, your human nature, bent on trying, rises to the challenge. What's the remedy for this all-too-common malady? Oswald Chambers, in his classic *My Utmost for His Highest*, wrote, "When God brings a time of waiting, and appears to be unresponsive, don't fill it with busyness, just wait. . . . If you have the slightest doubt, then he is not guiding."

The story of Abraham and Sarah illustrates the futility of trying to make a divine promise come about in your own timing. Tired of waiting for a son, Sarah took matters into her own hands. The result was disastrous. God's timetable always delivers an Isaac when the time is right.

I waited patiently for God to
help me; then he listened and
heard my cry. He lifted me
out of the pit of despair, out
from the bog and the mire,
and set my feet on a hard,
firm path, and steadied me
as I walked along.

PSALM 40:1–2 TLB

Slow me down, God,
when I am in a hurry and
you are not. Help me
walk with you, not ahead
of you. Teach me to plant
the seed and leave the
harvest to you.
Amen.

# PRAISE IN THE EVENING

*Oh, bless the LORD, all you servants of the LORD, you who serve as night watchmen in the house of the LORD.*

PSALM 134:1 NLT

The night sky, stitched with a pattern of glittering stars, hangs like a dark quilt over the landscape when viewed in the country. Without competition from city lights, the stars appear brighter and much more numerous. Shooting stars dart toward earth every now and then, and you wonder why you missed out for so long on this cosmic slide show.

If the cosmos could sing, the galaxies would rise up to praise their maker. Nighttime rituals, whether of stars or human beings, mark the end of the day and set the stage for reverence. Like the night watchmen who guarded Israel's temple, you are drawn to quiet praise and thankfulness for all God's goodness. And even when words fail you, a silent praise speaks for you deep within your heart.

I will bless the LORD who has counseled me; Indeed, my mind instructs me in the night. I have set the LORD continually before me; Because He is at my right hand, I will not be shaken.

PSALM 16:7–8 NASB

I bow in reverence, God, for the holiness of everything you created. When you made the world, you really had your mind on your work. Amen.

# THE AMAZING GRACE OF GOD

*He raises the poor from the dust, and lifts the needy from the ash heap, to make them sit with princes, with the princes of his people.*

PSALM 113:7–8 NRSV

God is constantly on the lookout, ready to rescue his beloved—you—whenever you fall or falter. Scripture says that he bends down from heaven to deal in the affairs of humankind—your affairs—lifting you up when you're on the ash heap of life. He not only lifts you from the dirt, he sets you in places of healing and favor, where your heart is strengthened and your spirit is renewed.

Though you may not always be aware of it, God pours his grace out on your life day after day, year after year. His grace marks your steps and directs your course. Because of his goodness, you can never escape his notice—not even if you try. God cares for you and is always there for you.

I love the Lord because he hears my prayers and answers them. Because he bends down and listens, I will pray as long as I breathe!

PSALM 116:1–2 TLB

Thank you, dear God, for the grace I don't always deserve but get anyway. It is everywhere, this grace, and it speaks clearly of you. Amen.

# TRAVELING MERCIES

*When a person's steps follow the LORD, God is*
*pleased with his ways. If he stumbles, he will not*
*fall, because the LORD holds his hand.*

PSALM 37:23–24 NCV

Guide horses on group trail rides are seldom picked for their beauty. Instead, the

rancher chooses horses that
are surefooted and not likely
to stumble. The horses you
find most beautiful are known
for their refined breeding and
high spirits. But the plodding,
surefooted breeds have a high
reputation of dependability on the trail or in a
harness. Their work ethic is unmatched.

Life's journey is fraught with unexpected
twists and turns, and the risk of stumbling
ranks high on the list of road hazards. No
doubt the psalmist knew this, but he had the
boldness to pen words that comfort you centuries later: When God holds you by the hand,
a stumble doesn't result in a fall. With his supporting arm, you catch your footing and continue surefooted along the trail.

Thou hast also given me the shield of thy salvation: and thy right hand hath holden me up, and thy gentleness hath made me great. Thou hast enlarged my steps under me, that my feet did not slip.

PSALM 18:35–36 KJV

Thank you, God, for my roots that sink deep into your promises. Keep me building always on rock, never on sand. Make me secure as I surrender to you. Amen.

# faith hope

moments of peace in the presence of God

*love*

One thing I ask of the LORD, this is what I seek: that I may dwell in the house of the LORD all the days of my life, to gaze upon the beauty of the LORD and to seek him in his temple.

PSALM 27:4 NIV

*beauty*

# GROWING WISER

*Thou through thy commandments has made me wiser than mine enemies: for they are ever with me. I have more understanding than all my teachers: for thy testimonies are my meditation.*

PSALM 119:98–99 KJV

The passing down of wisdom from parent to child, like cultural links in ancestral succession, gives character a chance to take root in each new generation. If watered, nourished, and pruned regularly, this heritage seedling will grow into a beautiful tree—broad, tall, and capable of withstanding the forces of nature and contributing to its environment. Its canopy of shade will protect all those who gather under its leafy branches. So also does a child grow into and then give back his or her wisdom.

Wisdom shows up best, not in the things you choose, but in the things you don't choose. That's when your legacy comes into fruition. With God as your gardener, you flourish in the place where he plants you, enriching your own life and the lives of others.

A good person speaks with wisdom, and he says what is fair. The teachings of his God are in his heart, so he does not fail to keep them.

PSALM 37:30–31 NCV

Dear God, give me wisdom to know what to look over and what to overlook. Teach me that the greatest wisdom is a loving heart and, when I am afraid, make me wise beyond my fears.
Amen.

# DIVINE NOURISHMENT

*You serve me a six-course dinner right in front of my enemies. You revive my drooping head; my cup brims with blessing.*

PSALM 23:5 THE MESSAGE

Food gives you the energy to keep going. There's no sign more welcome at the end of a long day on the road than RESTAURANT. Turning in, you anticipate the satisfying meal that waits inside. Cool water, maybe with lemon. Fresh garden salad. Hot bread or rolls. Tasty entrée. Two or three veggies. Perhaps a satisfying dessert. Once filled, you are revived and fortified for the next leg of your journey.

In the same way, God allows you to fill up from time spent with him. If your day is rushed and stressed, you may only have time for brief snacks—a hurried prayer, a verse you've memorized—and even then God stokes your spiritual energy. But once you settle in for a full-course spiritual meal, you realize what you've been missing and eat heartily.

My soul longs, indeed it
faints for the courts of
the LORD; my heart and
my flesh sing for joy to
the living God.

PSALM 84:2 NRSV

Move in me, dear God,
that I may see life from
your point of view. May
my spirit listen to your
Spirit in all things. Make
me each day more aware
of your presence.

Amen.

# TAKING REFUGE IN STRENGTH

*Incline your ear to me; rescue me speedily. Be a rock of refuge for me, a strong fortress to save me.*

PSALM 31:2 NRSV

Lighthouses are pictures of steadfastness. Battered by hurricane-force gales, pelted by sea  spray, and baked by the sun, those stone giants cling year after year to the coastline. They stand sometimes for centuries, and they are fascinating. A favorite with artists and photographers, lighthouses come to mind when you think of words like refuge, strong, or fortress, words that were used to describe God when David penned the thirty-first psalm.

Lighthouses not only stand against the elements and offer a stark beauty to the seascape, but their whole purpose is to save lives. They guide ships to safety by throwing light out into the night, beckoning the captains to shore. In a similar way, you might easily stray into dangerous waters if not for God's light thrown on your path.

My honor and salvation come from God. He is my mighty rock and my protection. People, trust God all the time. Tell him all your problems, because God is our protection.

PSALM 62:7–8 NCV

Dear God, may I listen for your guidance in the soft whispers and feel it in the gentle nudges of everyday life. Help me follow your light when I know it comes from you. Amen.

# DISTINCT AND BEAUTIFUL

*Arise, O LORD! O God, lift up Your hand! Do not forget the humble.*

PSALM 10:12 NKJV

Back in the days when mothers routinely sewed their children's clothes, dressmaking was a big event, especially when the dresses were cut from a particularly beautiful piece of cloth that had been set aside for Easter. A girl would watch eagerly as her mother's fingers transformed the fabric into a brand-new dress with the girl's very own dimensions.

Sometimes the excitement could fade, however, when a girl realized her sisters' dresses were not only going to be made from the same cloth, but they would be made from the same pattern as well. Then the mother would add a little touch that made each dress distinct—a lace collar, a scalloped edge, or a looping rickrack design. Though simple, the dresses were masterpieces—distinct and beautiful for each girl.

The LORD is King forever and ever; Nations have perished from His land.
O LORD, You have heard the desire of the humble; You will strengthen their heart, You will incline Your ear.

PSALM 10:16–17 NASB

Dear God, keep my eyes on Jesus, who refused to turn stones into bread, jump from great heights, or take over the rule of earthly kingdoms. Amen.

# HIDDEN IN THE SECRET PLACE

*Thou art my hiding place; thou shalt preserve me from trouble; thou shalt compass me about with songs of deliverance.*

PSALM 32:7 KJV

A secret childhood hiding place can be so vivid in your memory that at times it flashes back in Technicolor. Perhaps your hiding place was the broad branch of a tree where you could perch unseen thanks to the cover of a thousand green leaves. Or perhaps it was a shallow cave cut into the side of a slope or a small glade hidden behind a willow tree that formed a leafy curtain. You felt safe in your secret place—wonderfully alone, yet not fearful. You could go there anytime you wanted to.

Years later, God still hides you in the secret place of his protection. Though God's secret place is not tangible with leafy borders, your spirit recognizes at once how real this wonderful hiding place is. And you are at peace.

Rescue me from my enemies,
O Lord, for I hide myself in
you. Teach me to do your
will, for you are my God;
may your good Spirit lead
me on level ground.

Psalm 143:9–10 niv

Even when I can't see you,
O God, I know you are
there because you have
always been there. I cannot
remember a time you were
not present in my life, and
I thank you for that.
Amen.

# NATURE: GOD'S HERALD

*What a rich harvest your goodness provides!*
*Wherever you go there is plenty.*

PSALM 65:11 GNT

Young schoolchildren often take nature walks with brown paper bags in hand. As they set out on the trail, a teacher instructs them to bring back as many intriguing bits of nature as they can find: an acorn, a brightly colored leaf, a pine needle, a flower bud, an empty cocoon, an interesting pebble, a piece of bark.

As adults you may not venture outdoors with a bag in hand, but like children you can stop and marvel at God's fingerprint on the world around you. You see it everywhere you look in nature, from the intricacy of the filament and anther of a flower stamen to the watercolor brilliance of a sunset. Apart from the glory of nature, you also see God's artistic expression in his crowning achievement in creation: each other.

He covers the heavens with clouds, sends down the showers, and makes the green grass grow in mountain pastures. He feeds the wild animals, and the young ravens cry to him for food.

PSALM 147:8–9 TLB

Thank you for the world, dear God, a mighty volume wherein you declare yourself. I see your signature everywhere on the garments of what you have made. Amen.

# JOY OF THE BRIDEGROOM

*The sun comes out like a bridegroom from his bed-room. It rejoices like an athlete eager to run a race.*
PSALM 19:5 NCV

The above verse paints a word-picture of a new day bursting forth into the world with the joy and vigor of a bridegroom fresh from his wedding chamber. The anticipation of a new day is like the joy of an athlete ready to go. In the brightness, you sense God pouring out an unquenchable love.

Each new day bears God's stamp of approval that he sees in his creation. Each new day is delivered to you like a wrapped package that contains the gift of life. The very air you breathe bears witness to his overwhelming kindness toward you. Let every sunrise remind you of the unique opportunity to praise him. Let every race or athletic competition remind you of your praiseworthy God. There will never be another day just like today.

The LORD God is a sun and
shield: the LORD will give
grace and glory: no good
thing will he withhold from
them that walk uprightly.
O LORD of hosts, blessed is
the man that trusteth in thee.

PSALM 84:11–12 KJV

God, thank you for those
small daily happenings that
make life so spectacular.
Help me celebrate the
holiness of the common day.
Amen.

# THE BLESSINGS
# OF LONG LIFE

*The righteous flourish like the palm tree, and grow
like a cedar in Lebanon. . . . In old age they still
produce fruit.*

PSALM 92:12, 14 NRSV

Occasionally you may spot an elderly cou-
ple holding hands and gazing into each other's

eyes like newlyweds. *What's
their secret?* you wonder. If you
investigate a little more deeply,
you'll usually find two people
who are lifelong examples of
the second greatest command-
ment: Love your neighbor [or spouse] as yourself. Time has etched deep lines on their faces
and stooped their bodies, and yet their spirits
remain sound and supple—and as full of life as
when they first caught sight of each other and
recognized a kindred spirit.

Although you may long for a fairy-tale
romance that requires no effort, you often find
that the quintessential ingredient to every good
relationship is, after all, a servant's heart, each
person holding out the light of Christ for the
other as they journey together throughout life.

He will call upon me, and I will answer him; I will be with him in trouble, I will deliver him and honor him. With long life will I satisfy him and show him my salvation.

PSALM 91:15–16 NIV

Everything I know, O God, I know because I love. To love is to live, and to live is to love. Thank you for loving me in Jesus Christ. Amen.

# REASON FOR REJOICING

*O sing to the LORD a new song, For He has done wonderful things, His right hand and His holy arm have gained the victory for Him.*

PSALM 98:1 NASB

The giant oak tree outside the bedroom window was home to a vocal mockingbird. In the silver darkness just before dawn, the bird would throat up, mimicking the songs of other birds and singing a full repertoire of tunes. After the mockingbird had whistled its way through every last one, it would start all over again, like a CD stuck on continuous play. At first nearby residents considered the repetitive singing loud and obnoxious. Something would have to be done. Then they realized that the mockingbird's predawn song made them smile. In the end, listeners thought that it was a rare treat to wake to the sound of singing so vibrant that it stirred the neighborhood to spirited wakefulness.

Who but God could stir the mockingbird to such a songfest, day in and day out?

Hallelujah! Yes, let his people praise him as they stand in his Temple courts. Praise the Lord because he is so good; sing to his wonderful name.

PSALM 135:1–3 TLB

Dear God, help me not to sin by failing to rejoice in all you are to me and all you give to me. May I not take any of the gifts of life for granted. Amen.

# SWEETER THAN HONEY

*How sweet are Your words to my taste, Sweeter than honey to my mouth!*

PSALM 119:103 NKJV

Curling up with a good novel on a quiet day is one of life's underrated pleasures. You open the pages, and the world around you fades away while you're drawn, willingly, into the story before you. The author's words weave their magic, changing you if only slightly.

Who can deny the power of words to inspire, to deflate, to encourage, to discourage, to help, to hurt? The psalmist found the words of God not bittersweet, as so much human-inspired language turns out to be, but "sweeter than honey." Unlike your own words, his words are always life-giving. Though you may find pleasure in other books, the one God wrote has the power to transform you from the inside out. No wonder this perennial bestseller has stood the test of time.

I will sing unto the LORD as long as I live: I will sing praise to my God while I have my being. My meditation of him shall be sweet: I will be glad in the LORD.

PSALM 104:33–34 KJV

Thank you, dear God, for the words of life you speak to me. By your words I am named and claimed. By your words I am held, molded, and sent out. Amen.

# GOD'S PERFECT PLAN

*Wait and trust the LORD. Don't be upset when others get rich or when someone else's plans succeed.*

PSALM 37:7 NCV

Why is it easier to grieve with those who grieve than to rejoice with those who rejoice? When someone else's dream comes true, you may feel genuine happiness for your friend, but deep inside a small voice may cry out, God, have you forgotten about me? You thank him for the good that he has brought into the lives of others but wait anxiously for the day when it will be your turn.

One Bible version records it this way: "Be still before the Lord and wait patiently for him" (NIV). God is never in a hurry, but so often you are. All things happen, not in due time, but in divine time. There's no need to hurry, after all. God has everything under control and right on schedule, in divine time.

I am counting on the LORD; yes, I am counting on him. I have put my hope in his word. I long for the LORD more than sentries long for the dawn, yes, more than sentries for the dawn.

PSALM 130:5–6 NLT

I thank you, O God, for time I receive as a gift from you. May I honor each precious minute and use the time you give me as a way to bless your children.

Amen.

# THE MESSAGE IN THE GATES

*Lift up your heads, O ye gates; and be ye lift up, ye everlasting doors; and the King of glory shall come in.*

PSALM 24:7 KJV

Elaborate gates frame the walled city of Jerusalem. The gates still retain a noble look today, thousands of years after their construction. Though you will pass through thousands of gates and doors in your lifetime, you may not have stopped to consider what they signify. Gates and doorways are points of entry as well as points of exit. They allow people and objects to come in and go out. Gates and doorways protect and defend; they include and exclude. They guard against unwanted ingress or egress.

What about the doorway to your heart. Do you open your heart to others or do you keep it closed? When you let people enter, what do they find? Do they sense your welcome and peace? Do they know instinctively that God's Spirit dwells there?

Enter into his gates with thanksgiving, and into his courts with praise: be thankful unto him, and bless his name. For the LORD is good; his mercy is everlasting; and his truth endureth to all generations.

PSALM 100:4–5 KJV

Dear God, I know that at the heart of every problem is a problem of the heart. Make my heart a pure and welcoming place. Come into my heart now. Amen.

# LORD OF THE NIGHT

*Even the darkness is not dark to you; the night is as bright as the day, for darkness is as light to you.*

PSALM 139:12 NRSV

Waking up in the wee hours of the night, you find that all is still and black as pitch. As you walk to the refrigerator for a drink, your eye peeks outside at the night sky, the backyard, and the woods that fringe the edge of the lawn. What is it about nighttime that calls the spirit toward fear or peace, anxiety or calm?

When he penned the lines of Psalm 139, David prefaced them with these rhetorical questions: Where could I go from your Spirit? Or where could I flee from your presence? David knew that even the darkness could not hide him from God's watchful eyes and blanketing care. The darkness need not hold fear for you; God always watches over you. And that is reason enough to find peace in the night.

By day the LORD directs his
love, at night his song is
with me—a prayer to the
God of my life.

PSALM 42:8 NIV

Dear God, may I walk
straight into my darkness
and trust that your light
will chase it away. And
when darkness comes
again, may I remember
what I learned in the light.
Amen.

# LORD OF THE LIGHT

*O Lord my God, how great you are! You are robed with honor and with majesty and light!*

PSALM 104:1–2 TLB

Light has the power to refresh and revitalize you. After the long stretch of night, the sun's morning rays are a welcome sight as they push through the trees and make dappled patterns on the ground. In a very real and verifiable sense, your body responds to sunlight. Sunlight helps set your biological clock, lift your mood and immune system, and even produce vitamin D to keep you strong and well and functioning properly.

Scripture assures you that God is "robed with majesty and light." God, the one who burst onto the scene of early creation with light—the sun by day, the moon and stars by night—fills you with another, more stirring kind of light when you spend time with him. God fills you with the light of his goodness.

If I rise with the sun in the east and settle in the west beyond the sea, even there you would guide me. With your right hand you would hold me.

PSALM 139:9–10 NCV

When I am unable to live in the light you are, dear God, help me walk toward it. I know it is there to reveal your love and show me the way I am to walk.
Amen.

faith hope

moments of peace in the presence of God

*love*

*Bless the LORD, O
my soul, and do not
forget all his benefits.*
PSALM 103:2 NRSV

*blessings*

# RENEWED VIGOR

*Who satisfies your mouth with good things,*
*So that your youth is renewed like the eagle's.*

PSALM 103:5 NKJV

Who hasn't felt the downward drag of fatigue, whether induced by age, stress, or a bout

of illness? When your body lacks vigor, you long for—and remember—the feeling of vitality more than ever. And in these times you recall that God promised to renew your youth like the eagle's.

When you watch an eagle fly, you can see how effortlessly it seems to navigate the sky. Though equipped with wings that can reach ninety inches wide, this powerful bird glides for long distances on columns of rising air called thermals. In the same way, God carries you on the strength of his wings, giving you spiritual, emotional, and physical vitality when you most need it. As you ride his divine thermals, you remember once again how you thrive in his care.

Pushed to the wall, I called to GOD; from the wide open spaces, he answered. GOD's now at my side and I'm not afraid; who would dare lay a hand on me? GOD's my strong champion; I flick off my enemies like flies.

PSALM 118:5–7 THE MESSAGE

Dear God, you enable me to swim strongly in deep water. You help me rise above whatever pulls me down. Thank you. Amen.

# TEARS IN A BOTTLE

*Thou tellest my wanderings: put thou my tears into thy bottle: are they not in thy book?*

PSALM 56:8 KJV

The verse above paints a word-picture that is at once hard to believe and awe-inspiring.

Like a woman who saves a rare perfume in a bottle, God stores your tears in his bottle and records them in his book. The divine book-keeper chronicles every twist and turn you take down the path of life.

When David wrote this psalm, he was running for his life from King Saul's men. His cry to the Lord did not fall on deaf ears; God heard him. His tears were not wasted; God knew and cared about them. Your tears won't be wasted either. Though you may not be in mortal danger, it's a comfort to know that God notes your every teardrop, just as he notices when one tiny sparrow falls from a tree.

LORD, my Rock, I call out to you for help. Do not be deaf to me. If you are silent, I will be like those in the grave. Hear the sound of my prayer, when I cry out to you for help. I raise my hands toward your Most Holy Place.

PSALM 28:1–2 NCV

Cushion me, dear God, when I am on pins and needles. I know you can clear the darkest sky and bring day to night. Amen.

# PERSONAL MEMORIALS

*Come and hear, all you who fear God, and I will tell what he has done for me.*

PSALM 66:16 NRSV

The art of storytelling, no doubt, dates back to the Garden of Eden, and for good reason. Most people enjoy the pleasure factor of a good story, and you probably do as well. Even more, however, you enjoy the purpose—and the memories—that you find in stories. Through oral histories you learn what went before you, and through them you pass on what has happened in your own life stories so that time will not erase your experiences.

Erecting personal memorials of your life—stories, photo albums, family traditions, prayer journals, and the like—commemorates the blessings that come your way. When you "tell of what he has done," you are twice blessed: in seeing the joy it brings to others and in the reliving of your story.

Parents will tell their children
what you have done. They will
retell your mighty acts, wonderful majesty, and glory. And
I will think about your miracles. They will tell about the
amazing things you do, and I
will tell how great you are.

PSALM 145:4–6 NCV

Praise you, God, for the story
you write in my life, the story
of how you save me because
you love me. Thank you for
the good news of this story.
Amen.

# GOD'S AWESOME DEEDS

*You faithfully answer our prayers with awesome deeds, O God our savior. You are the hope of everyone on earth, even those who sail on distant seas.*

PSALM 65:5 NLT

In ancient times, before people knew that the earth is round, ancient seamen thought that if they sailed too far and skirted too close to the horizon, they would fall off the edge of the earth. You may sometimes feel that your life feels much the same way. You may struggle to navigate through choppy waters and imagine the worst. But the next time you experience this kind of disquietude and fretfulness, call out to God for guidance. He will surprise you with awesome deeds—answers to prayer that surpass your understanding.

No matter what happens today, you can know that your life is in the same hands that hold the earth steady on its axis. God is faithful to act, to answer prayers, and to perform his amazing feats—all in his perfect timing.

In you our ancestors trusted;
they trusted, and you delivered them. To you they cried,
and were saved; in you they
trusted, and were not
put to shame.

Psalm 22:4–5 NRSV

You never go on strike in
my life, dear God. You
are always there to love,
protect, and renew me. I
live and move in you.
Amen.

# WORDS THAT RESTORE

*I rejoice at Your word As one who finds great treasure.*

PSALM 119:162 NKJV

At the end of Mark Twain's classic *Tom Sawyer,* the boy-hero of Hannibal, Missouri, uncovers a treasure buried in the cavern that nearly claimed his life. The town rejoices at Tom's good fortune, and you, the reader, get to peek over his shoulder, vicariously experiencing the thrill of finding something of great worth long buried.

That's just the sort of word-picture that David painted in Psalm 119. Like a newly discovered treasure, God's words fill you with joy and the promise of lifelong provision, no matter how many times you read them. When you uncover this cache of riches, you become heir of a fortune that transcends earthly values. To your surprise, you find that for the first time in your life your cup runs over, just as the psalmist said it would.

Your goodness continues forever, and your teachings are
true. I have had troubles and
misery, but I love your commands. Your rules are always
good. Help me understand
so I can live.

PSALM 119:142–144 NCV

Through your word of
encouragement, dear God, I
become myself. Thank you
for looking far enough in me
to see strengths and skills I
don't know are there.
Amen.

# JOY IN LOWLY TASKS

*A single day spent in your Temple is better than a thousand anywhere else! I would rather be a doorman of the Temple of my God than live in palaces of wickedness.*

PSALM 84:10 TLB

Whether it's pausing to wipe peanut butter from a child's face or picking up stray bits of trash in a neighbor's yard, your little deeds of kindness speak a love language all their own—the language of God's love. In these mundane tasks you find a simple kind of joy that comes from giving without strings attached. That joy is its own reward.

Translated to a modern setting, this psalm might celebrate the church sexton who vacuums the carpet every week, the altar guild member who cleans and presses the altar linens, or the teenage boy who pulls weeds from the church's flower bed. Though these jobs carry little prestige, the faithful performance of them doesn't go unnoticed by God. When you work for him, you are in the employment of the King.

I will sing of your love and fairness; LORD, I will sing praises to you. I will be careful to live an innocent life. When will you come to me? I will live an innocent life in my house.

PSALM 101:1–2 NCV

Dear God, when I play second fiddle may I play it well for you. When I am called on to be a stand-in, may I stand tall and bless your holy name.
Amen.

# THE TEACHABLE HEART

*Teach me thy way, O LORD; I will walk in thy truth: unite my heart to fear thy name.*

PSALM 86:11 KJV

Saint Augustine once wrote to a young pupil, "Education is the food of youth, the delight of old age, the ornament of prosperity, the refuge and comfort of adversity, and the provocation to grace in the soul." No matter how much traditional education you get, however, it can't compare with the sort of schooling that God gives.

It has been said that life is a classroom and that God is your constant teacher. A teacher can only teach a willing pupil, however, so you must yield to God's authority. Through the patient repetition of life's lessons and a gentle and not-so-gentle prodding, God proves to be a schoolmaster who always transforms those who submit to his teaching. Like the psalmist, when you learn his way you will walk in his truth.

Oh, the joys of those who do not follow the advice of the wicked, or stand around with sinners, or join in with scoffers. But they delight in doing everything the LORD wants; day and night they think about his law.

PSALM 1:1–2 NLT

Thank you, dear God, for the teachers you send me. When they come to teach, may I be ready to learn. In what they say, may I hear you speak to me.
Amen.

# GOD'S STRENGTH IS ENOUGH

*Powerful is your arm! Strong is your hand! Your right hand is lifted high in glorious strength.*

PSALM 89:13 NLT

To small children, an adult must look like a giant. You loom over them and stoop down to pick them up in your arms. In the instant you do, however, your intimidating strength blurs into a single gesture of tenderness. Sometimes that's how you see God—vast and mighty and towering in strength high above you. The moment he folds you in his arms, however, you remember that he is, after all, your loving God.

When you grow weak and afraid, the image of God's strong arms brings a fresh reminder of his nearness. God is quick to save you when you call on him, and he promises to keep you in the palm of his hand. There, safe in his grasp, you find the courage and strength to do whatever he asks of you.

With a strong hand, and
with a stretched out arm: for
his mercy endureth for ever.
To him which divided the
Red sea into parts: for his
mercy endureth for ever.

PSALM 136:12–13 KJV

You are able, dear God, to
do far more with me than I
am able to do with myself.
I trust your power, seek
your wisdom, and surren-
der to your leading.
Amen.

# GOD'S ANSWER IS ON THE WAY

*The righteous cry out, and the LORD hears,*
*And delivers them out of all their troubles.*

PSALM 34:17 NKJV

Camping out deep in the woods, you notice that night falls quickly and thickly. The darkness wraps everything in its blanket of black, making a flashlight the camper's best friend in an emergency. The camper's watch snags on the foliage, snapping from his wrist, so he retraces his steps with the light beamed out in front of him, illuminating the ground. He hears rustling in the bushes and shines the flashlight in that direction, making light circles, searching for the source.

In a similar way, your heart beams out into the darkness, calling to God when you're troubled or simply in need of an answer. He promises that when you search for him, you will find him. Often what you find is that his answer is already on the way.

Rise up! Be our help, And
redeem us for the sake of
your lovingkindness.

PSALM 44:26 NASB

Dear God, I stand on tiptoe
as I wait for your answer to
my prayers. When I hear
from you, it will be more
than worth the wait.
Amen.

# GOD'S MERCY

*As parents feel for their children, GOD feels for those who fear him. He knows us inside and out, keeps in mind that we're made of mud.*

PSALM 103:13–14 THE MESSAGE

Kermit Roosevelt, the son of Teddy Roosevelt, once wrote, "The great man never loses his child's heart. What is true of the Kingdom of God must also be true in the affairs of men." If a loving earthly father feels for his children, how much more is God moved with compassion for you? This psalm captures God's tender thoughts toward you. Other versions say that he remembers that people are dust; God knows human weakness.

Can mud and dust ever have any hope of attaining Godlikeness? The question needs no answer because you know all too well your own shortcomings. The miracle of life, breathed into your body clay, opens the doorway to something even more miraculous, if you but reach out and take it: God's own life in you.

Who can forget the wonders
he performs? How gracious
and merciful is our LORD!
He gives food to those who
trust him; he always remembers
his covenant.

PSALM 111:4–5 NLT

Thank you, dear God, for
the margin of error you
allow me. Thank you for
your doors of mercy that
are always open.
Amen.

# A BOUNTIFUL CROP

*They sowed fields and planted vineyards that yield-
ed a fruitful harvest; he blessed them, and their
numbers greatly increased, and he did not let their
herds diminish.*

PSALM 107:37 NIV

American writer George
Grant wrote a letter home to his
wife about what he called "one of
London's most delightful gardens"
nestled within the tiny churchyard
of Saint Mary's parish. Most
intriguing of all was a bronze
plaque in one corner that declared
A GOOD THEOLOGY WILL INVARIABLY PRODUCE
A GOOD GARDEN.

Grant was at first amused by the epigram,
but he later realized that the words conveyed
what he called a scriptural world-view: A solid
theology always takes into consideration the link
between the profound and the ordinary. Like
tending a garden, Grant said that cultivating a
balanced view of God involves "both the drudg-
ery of daily labor and the high ideals of faith,
hope, and love. But the results are always worth
the extra effort."

*E*very one of these depends
on you to give them daily
food. You supply it, and they
gather it. You open wide
your hand to feed them and
they are satisfied with all
your bountiful provision.

PSALM 104:27–28 TLB

Thank you, God, for the
accomplishments of small
beginnings. Thank you for
great journeys from first
steps and large harvests
from tiny seeds.
Amen.

# A TIME TO BE LOUD

*Hallelujah! I give thanks to GOD with everything I've got— Wherever good people gather, and in the congregation.*

PSALM 111:1 THE MESSAGE

Sometimes your joy is so tangible you feel you might burst if you don't get it out. At those times, you may want to climb to the rooftop and shout out the goodness of God. All creation praises him, from the crickets' nighttime chorus to the wind's whistling through the eaves. And if you ceased to proclaim his goodness, Scripture says that the miraculous would take place: The rocks themselves would cry out. Imagine such a sound—a true rock concert of praise.

There's a time and place for quiet, meditative faith. There's a time and place for silent prayer. There's a time and place for soft, worshipful singing. And there's a time and place to praise God with all the gusto you can muster. Yes, there is a time to be loud.

Praise the LORD! Praise, O
servants of the LORD. Praise
the name of the LORD.
Blessed be the name of the
LORD From this time forth
and forever.

PSALM 113:1–2 NASB

I can't say enough praises
to you, God, for the blessings of my life. They spill
out all around me. I raise
my praise to you.
Amen.

# ALONG THE FOOTPATH

*Make me go in the path of thy commandments;*
*for therein do I delight.*

PSALM 119:35 KJV

In his poem "The Road Not Taken," Robert Frost wrote about two paths that diverge in a wood and how he chose the "one less traveled by." He ended the poem with these words: "and that has made all the difference." Similarly, you may ponder what may have happened if you had veered down another life path. Ultimately, however, it's the path taken that molds you into the person you turned out to be—for better or for worse. How blessed you are when you choose the path that leads to God.

Just as a footpath through the woods winds its way past twisting roots and low-hanging branches, the narrow way that leads to God may be full of obstacles. Someday you'll be able to look back and rejoice over the road not taken.

I will follow your rules forever, because they make me
happy. I will try to do what
you demand forever,
until the end.

PSALM 119:111–112 NCV

Dear God, I choose the
abundant life you offer
and the eternal life you
promise. I have decided to
follow you in all things.
Amen.

# A LASTING HERITAGE

*The LORD is the portion of mine inheritance and of my cup: thou maintainest my lot. The lines are fallen unto me in pleasant places; yea, I have a good inheritance.*

PSALM 16:5–6 KJV

The word *inheritance* denotes good things to come, a promise of unexpected blessings. You would be delighted to hear that a distant relative had willed property or wealth to you. Just the knowledge that you had been chosen, hand-picked to receive the blessing, would trigger a rush of feeling.

The psalmist rejoiced that the God who hung the stars in their places was his inheritance, that the one who spoke the world into existence was his portion. The same is true for you when you are the child of God. Though God owns all the cattle on all the hills, as his heir you claim riches of another kind—and the best gift is still to come, on the day when you will see him face to face.

The LORD will not cast off
his people, neither will he
forsake his inheritance.

PSALM 94:14 KJV

God, I am your grateful
child who loves and
serves you. Thank you for
the rich inheritance of
your blessings in my life.
Amen.

# WHOLESOME PRESERVATIVES

*The LORD shall preserve thee from all evil: he shall
preserve thy soul. The LORD shall preserve thy
going out and thy coming in from this time forth,
and even for evermore.*

PSALM 121:7–8 KJV

Patrick was sold into slavery as a teenager
when marauding Irishmen raid-
ed the English coastal regions
where he lived. During his years
as a slave, this son of a deacon
turned to God with zeal. After
escaping to England, he
dreamed that an Irishman begged him to return
and preach to his countrymen. Patrick did return
to Ireland as a missionary and became the
Emerald Isle's most beloved saint—Saint Patrick.

We read much about the preservatives that
go into your food, stripping them of their organic
value. One kind of preservative, however, is good
for your body as well as your soul: God. He protects you from evil and preserves your "going out"
and "coming in." As Patrick discovered, what
comes disguised as evil, God often uses for good.

You both precede and follow me. You place your hand of blessing on my head. Such knowledge is too wonderful for me, too great for me to know! I can never escape from your spirit! I can never get away from your presence!

PSALM 139:5–7 NLT

I take no step, God, you do not see. Nothing about me eludes you. Nothing I think, say, or do escapes your attention.

Amen.

# SOMEONE BETTER THAN BEFORE

*The LORD is gracious, and full of compassion; slow to anger, and of great mercy.*

PSALM 145:8 KJV

The caterpillar doesn't argue that it would rather be a butterfly. It simply submits to the plan that God created for it and curls up inside the cocoon when the time comes for the miracle to take place. And what a miracle it is. When the transformation is complete, a different creature—different in form and different in ability—emerges from the cocoon and flies away to begin its new life with wings.

In his mercy, God transforms you as well—if you let him. He exchanges your impatience for grace and your anger for compassion. After his work is complete in you, you emerge as someone better than you were before. With God's love and grace inside you, you, like him, become slow to anger and quick to love.

His anger endureth but a
moment; in his favour is
life: weeping may endure
for a night, but joy
cometh in the morning.

PSALM 30:5 KJV

Dear God, make love the
reason for my living and the
aim of my life. I know that
when I love I have your
heart and am in your will.
Amen.

# GOD'S NIGHT WATCH

*I will lie down and sleep in peace, for you alone, O*
*LORD, make me dwell in safety.*

PSALM 4:8 NIV

A good night's sleep is one of those small
blessings that is often taken for
granted until you lose it, tossing
fitfully, unable to relax your guard.
Peaceful sleep? David could
appreciate it more than the average
person. He was a man who slept in
caves while on the run from a king
with murderous intent. Yet even in
the midst of life-threatening danger, his heart
was at peace because he knew that God alone
made him dwell in safety.

No deadbolt or bar at the window can
replace the serenity that comes from trusting
God for your security. Because of his night
watch over you, you can crawl into bed and
sleep the deep slumber of a child, comforted by
the knowledge that God is guarding you body
and soul.

I can lie down and go to sleep, and I will wake up again, because the LORD gives me strength.

PSALM 3:5 NCV

I know, dear Lord, that you guide me and that you provide for me. Thank you for meeting my needs and for blessing my deeds. Amen.

# SKILLFULLY WROUGHT

*Thank you for making me so wonderfully complex! Your workmanship is marvelous—and how well I know it.*

PSALM 139:14 NLT

A mirror can be your best friend or your worst enemy. Sometimes you may feel that you're looking into a fun-house mirror, seeing a caricature of who you are. But the special quality that makes you who you are is found in no other human being on earth. Maybe it's the way you tilt your head when you talk, or the way you burst into laughter at unexpected moments. Perhaps others see a sparkle in your eyes that you never knew was there. Beyond the physical, you possess qualities that make you a true original. God said so, and his workmanship is marvelous.

When you glimpse a newborn baby, you take note of his tiny fingernails, his very small eyebrows. God crafted every detail of that newborn babe, just as he created every detail of you.

That our sons may be as plants grown up in their youth; that our daughters may be as corner stones, polished after the similitude of a palace.

PSALM 144:12 KJV

Help me, God, to see myself as you see me and believe in myself as you believe in me. May I live up to the potential you placed in me.
Amen.

faith hope

moments of peace in the presence of God